THE NEW YORK WRITER'S SOURCE BOOK

**Department of Cultural Affairs
City of New York**

ADDISON-WESLEY PUBLISHING COMPANY
Reading, Massachusetts •Menlo Park, California
London •Amsterdam •Don Mills, Ontario •Sydney

Library of Congress Cataloging in Publication Data
Main entry under title:

The New York writer's source book.

    First ed.: New York, N.Y.: Dept. of Cultural
Affairs, City of New York, 1981.
    Bibliography: p.
    Includes index.
    1. Authorship—Societies, etc.—Directories.
2. Authorship—Handbooks, manuals, etc. I. New York
(N.Y.). Dept. of Cultural Affairs. II. Title:
New York writer's sourcebook.
PN121.N53   1983   808′.02′0257471   83–5978
ISBN 0–201–06024–8

Cover design by Seymour Chwast
Interior design by Pedro A. Noa, Merlin Communications, Inc.

ABCDEFGHIJ-DO-86543
First printing, June 1983

CONTENTS

Foreword by Henry Geldzahler vii
Preface by Claire Tankel 1
Introduction: Living and Writing in New York
          by Kenneth Koch 3

PART I. WRITERS' ORGANIZATIONS 9

1. Professional and Service Organizations 11
2. Guilds and Advocacy Groups 45
3. Women's and Minority Organizations 56
4. Community Councils 75
5. Information Clearinghouses 84

PART II. SPECIAL OPPORTUNITIES FOR WRITERS 93

6. Career Development and Job Options 95
7. Grants and Fellowships 107
8. Writers' Conferences in the Northeast 119
9. Graduate Writing Programs 125
10. Writers' Colonies and Writers' Rooms 137
11. Small Presses and Magazines 147
12. Readings: Live and Recorded 165

Appendixes
Special Issues in Developing a Writing Career 173
Annotated Filmography 176
Annotated Bibliography 179
Alphabetical Index of Organizations 185
Index of Organizations by Subject 187

FOREWORD

In a very real sense, the notion of "helping" artists is presumptuous. The things that artists do for the rest of us far outweigh the value of any assistance we can offer them. And yet, it is possible, in practical terms, if not to ease the path that artists must walk, at least to fill in the bigger potholes.

It is with this modest intention that the Department of Cultural Affairs conceived of a series of information manuals, handbooks that would succinctly and thoroughly describe the full range of services and service agencies available to the professional artist. Thus, in 1981, we published the first edition of *The Writer's New York City Source Book*. The book was well received, and encouraged by its success, we have revised and expanded its contents and, in order to secure a wider distribution, arranged for its publication by Addison-Wesley.

It is our hope that this book will be of service to writers throughout the country. For the most part, making art is a solitary task. We have attempted to provide access to a network consisting of other artists who work in the same discipline, organizations that provide services to artists, and information concerning employment, publication, and competitions. We believe that this source book will help every artist work more efficiently and with greater freedom.

I want to thank Claire Tankel, the original Director of our Arts Apprenticeship Program, who conceived of these books. Her energy and commitment to this project have been exemplary. A special thanks must also go to Marlene Hauser, a young writer who, as a student participant in the Arts Apprenticeship Program under the direction of Ms. Tankel, researched, organized, compiled, and prepared for printing the first edition of *The Writer's New York City Source Book*.

Henry Geldzahler, Commissioner
New York City Department of Cultural Affairs, 1978–1982

THE
NEW YORK
WRITER'S
SOURCE
BOOK

PREFACE

This book has grown out of the work I have done as the director of the Arts Apprenticeship Program of the New York City Department of Cultural Affairs. Over the years since 1974, I have worked with many writers, both established professionals and younger, would-be authors. I have noticed that writers, whatever their career level, expressed similar needs and concerns, including the need to earn money from writing; "a room of one's own," a fine and private place to practice a most private art; current information about publishers, especially the small presses; help with distribution; information about alternative job options that are both congenial and allied to writing.

We hope that this book will meet some of these needs or at least point the user in the right direction for finding further and more thorough information. By intention and design, this book is a source book rather than an encyclopedia. Writers using it will probably find just enough information on a service or an organization to enable them to ask intelligent questions; rarely will an entry provide a complete answer. We urge you to contact these organizations directly. Subscribing to one or more of the newsletters mentioned in this book (for example, the Poets & Writers publication *Coda* or the bulletin of the Association of Hispanic Arts) will serve as a valuable supplement to this book for most writers.

Although this book has been produced by an agency of New York City and the service and support organizations listed are based in New York City, we hope that it will nonetheless be of value to writers living in all parts of the country. Indeed, for those writers who do not live in or near large metropolitan areas or academic centers, a source book such as this may be particularly useful. Every attempt has been made to assure the accuracy of the information contained herein. Organizations and their services, however, can change as quickly as the times do. Also, despite our best efforts, we may have overlooked a valuable service or resource. We therefore welcome any suggestions, corrections, or additions that users of this book may have. Such comments should be addressed to the Arts Apprenticeship Program, Department of Cultural Affairs, 2 Columbus Circle, New York, New York 10019.

The Department of Cultural Affairs Arts Apprenticeship Program has received support over the years from a number of public and private agencies, including the National Endowment for the Arts, the Creative Artists in Public Service Program (CAPS), and the New York City Urban Corps Program.

The first version of the *New York Writer's Source Book* was supported in part with grants from Chemical Bank, Consolidated Edison, Newsweek, and the Print Center. Two highly creative artists also made important contributions in their work: Toshida Ide and Seymour Chwast, whose cover design and award-winning poster brought the book crucial visibility.

The following people made important contributions to this book and to the work of the Arts Apprenticeship Program: Henry Geldzahler, former Commissioner of the Department of Cultural Affairs; Randall Bourscheidt; Richard Bruno; Lisa Rubinstein and Scott Penney, who assisted in the research and writing; Karen Murgolo, our editor at Addison-Wesley; Elyse Reissman; Howard Rubinstein; Robert J. Vanni; Susan Rothschild; Ellen Liman; Clay Conley; Pearl Brooks; Pamela Gwynn; Peter Sylvester; George Melrod; Tim Williams; Jeanette Ingberman; Kathy Jason; Diane Maychick; and Barbara Singleton. Most important, I wish to thank my children, Josh and Joanna Tankel, for their constant support and inspiration.

Claire Tankel, Director
Arts Apprenticeship Program
Department of Cultural Affairs

Introduction: LIVING AND WRITING IN NEW YORK

The best introduction to this book might be autobiographical essays by ten or twenty writers, since every writer's experience is different. I was asked to write about mine, presumably with the hope that in some way what happened to one writer—in his attempts to write, to be published, to survive—would be useful either in its general outline or in some of its details.

From the time I was five, I liked to write. Verbal entertainment was popular in my house in Cincinnati, Ohio; when I told stories, made jokes, or made up poems, it was generally approved of. When I was fifteen, my Uncle Leo gave me an old red-covered edition of Shelley's *Collected Poems*, and I was a sort of Romantic poet until, at seventeen, I discovered modern poetry, chiefly in Louis Untermeyer's *Modern British and American Poetry*, in *New Directions Yearbooks*, and in *Poetry* magazine. I was greatly encouraged in my writing that year, and in my conversion to modernism by a high school English teacher named Katherine Lappa. At that time I began to write a lot of poems; I think I wrote almost every day. Then I was in the army and then at Harvard; before I went to Harvard I spent several months writing as much as I could, like William Carlos Williams. Once there, I studied writing with Delmore Schwartz, who told me to read Yeats. He also encouraged me to write verse plays. The first one I wrote that I liked, *Little Red Riding Hood*, was Yeats-like and full of gongs, dance gestures, and symbols.

I went to live in New York, where, aside from a few years in France and Italy and one year in Berkeley, California, I've lived ever since. I was writing and taking courses for an M.A. at Columbia. I met Jane Freilicher and Larry Rivers. John Ashbery, whom I had known at Harvard, and Frank O'Hara, whom I hadn't, came to New York. We five spent a great deal of time together. We were, for each other, a small but very good audience: available, exigent, enthusiastic. We felt full of talent. We were just about totally unpublished and unknown. Life was a little hard. Fortunately, we had each other. After a few years, by 1952 or 1953, I had a way of writing poems that seemed to me, more than any way I'd written before, really my own. I had the impression we were all, by that time, doing good new work. We poets spent time in the painters' studios. The painters, amid the heady smell of oil paint and turpentine, using up the sunlight the way we used the language, put a slash of green there, a spot of purple there, turned around and said, "Oh, well!" or "I think that's it!"

I think I was writing poems in a not wholly dissimilar way. On lucky days, new ideas every afternoon—or late morning—and new poems, or parts of a long poem, finished or unfinished, by night. I remember, in 1953, sitting every afternoon in the little apartment my wife, Janice, and I had on Charles Street, looking out the window and writing *When the Sun Tries to Go On*, a very long poem inspired by *War and Peace* and by my excitement about and slight misunderstanding of the French language. I was so excited by writing that poem that I had the illusion, several times, that I was going to die. Instead I called up Frank and read him parts of it; he read me part of his poem *Second Avenue*, which was almost as long. We were, he said, pleased by it, "burning up the wires." John, in revenge for, or in mockery of, our lengthiness, solemnly composed a one-line poem. A few days later, though, he wrote a long one. My friends and I collaborated with each other writing poems—many of these with certain things that had to go in every line (a city and a kind of drink, for example, or a statue). Frank came over one night and we had a "race," he at one typewriter, I at another, or not so much a race as a writing "against each other," with the clacking of the other's typewriter a source of inspiration. A little later we did painting-poetry collaborations, the first ones with Larry Rivers. There seemed to be so much "subject" that it hardly had to be thought of. The sound of a typewriter, the look of green paint suggested words, lines, ideas. The quality of all this work was certainly various—less so the absorbingness of doing it. As we grew older, were published more, and became otherwise involved, these friendships didn't end but, as far as our work was concerned, became less important.

To make money in the early fifties, Frank worked at the Museum of Modern Art, John at Oxford University Press; both, along with James Schuyler, also wrote art criticism. Supported by the G.I. Bill, which gave money to veterans for school, I studied as long as I could; then I taught. Our social life was each other and the painters. When our social group expanded, for years all the new people, except for

Barbara Guest, James Schuyler and Arnold Weinstein, were painters: Fairfield Porter, Grace Hartigan, Al Leslie, Mike Goldberg, Joan Mitchell, to name only a few. At night, at the Cedar Bar on University Place, while abstract expressionist painters, full of passion and theory, talked stormily or quietly, we listened (sometimes), drank, and showed each other new works. Painters, and particularly John Myers, who ran the De Nagy Art Gallery, also helped us to be published. Myers published first books by John, Frank, and me. He also put on our first plays. My book *Prints and Poems*, a collaboration with Nell Blaine, was a large-size twenty-page book containing poems and black-and-white and full-color woodblock prints. I think Nell and I each contributed $150 toward its publication. It had an "opening" at the De Nagy Gallery in 1951, with Nell's paintings on the walls. The book cost $5, which in 1951 was expensive. There were, in the early fifties, almost no poetry readings, at least not for poets so unknown as we were. I remember a very few group readings, in art galleries.

This was a great time, in New York, for painting. Sales and shows weren't yet what they would be, but they had begun, and the energy, the excitement, and the promise of the new painting were unmistakable. Poetry seemed in a different state. Pound, Williams, Stevens, and other great writers had been vaguely appropriated into an "establishment" run by the most conservative (we said "academic") of their descendants. The publications, the fellowships, the prizes were all theirs. Publicly, in any case, that was the situation. In fact, young poets were reading Whitman, Pasternak, Apollinaire, Rilke—and reading Pound and Williams on their own—and had already begun something new. Official recognition of the new poetry being written then didn't begin, really, till the late fifties, with the publication of Allen Ginsberg's *Howl*. *Howl* wasn't like the poetry my friends and I wrote, but it shared with our poetry an impressive unlikeness to what was considered good poetry.

So, in this personal and cultural situation in the fifties, we published where we could, which was not very many places. Like other artists, along with wanting to do good work, we wanted our work to be recognized. Our friendship, I think, helped us to write better; and we knew that someone liked what we wrote. Of course I wanted (as I presume they did also) for that liking to extend further than it did. While we were inspiring and criticizing each other's work, we sent things to magazines, entered contests, put together manuscripts for books. Often, if we published in a little magazine, it was in one connected in some way to art. Sometimes one of us would publish something in *Poetry* or the *Partisan Review*. Our collaborative books with painters came out when we were in our late twenties; our first books with regular publishers—Grove Press and Yale University Press—when we were in our middle thirties. In the late 1950s there were new magazines—*Yugen, Big Table, Evergreen Review*—that published us. At the end of the fifties, Harry Mathews started publishing *Locus Solus*, the first "New York School" magazine not connected to painting.

The play I wrote at Harvard, *Little Red Riding Hood*, was produced as part of a series called the Artists' Theatre at the Theatre De Lys in New York City in 1953. Grace Hartigan did the sets. Frank, John, and James Schuyler also did plays with artists. I loved hearing my words spoken on stage and seeing people acting them out. I liked writing plays, I think because, for one thing, it made me feel free of the lyrical "trap," the obligation to say one thing, stay on the subject, and that's it. In a play there could be everybody saying everything. Or close to it. I found that once an ingenious person got hold of them, the craziest things I had thought of could be put on stage. In my play *Guinevere* there is a stage direction "The world splits in two like an orange." Red Grooms was doing the sets, and I said that might be a hard moment for the set designer. "Oh, not at all," he said; "it's simple." Some plays I wrote specifically to be done with artworks: *The Construction of Boston* and *The Tingueley Machine Mystery*. The latter, performed at the Jewish Museum where Jean Tingueley had a show, featured Tingueley's machines as characters as well as humans. In these plays, and in a few others, I used my friends as actors. Other plays were done professionally. In the theater a writer often has to deal with people who are not primarily interested in literary art as he conceives it. Another difficulty is money and all that goes with that.

When I first wrote plays, out of the same verbal exhilaration that caused me to write poems, theater people said they weren't theatrical enough. If I spent time in the theater, I'd know what it was like and would be able to write for it better. This was true in one way and not in another. What they sometimes meant by theatrical, in fact, was conventional Broadway stuff, which I didn't want to know how to do. Being involved in some of my plays, though, going to rehearsal after rehearsal, especially to those of The Red Robins, which Don Sanders directed (in 1977 and 78) I did get ideas I wouldn't otherwise have had—for speeches, scenes, and even whole new plays. In these ideas, often, space, time, action, and all sorts of things that had to do with the stage were mixed up with the words.

6

When I was in high school and college and already knew I wanted to be a poet, I couldn't figure out what I could do to make money. I never wanted to try to live by my writing. I was afraid that then I wouldn't be able to write what I wanted to, and that the writing I did do would take up all my time. Fortunately, all those years on the G.I. Bill prepared me (officially) for college teaching. I found I liked teaching and also that it left me enough time to write poetry. One of the first courses I taught was at the New School, a poetry-writing workshop. I was interested in trying out certain ideas I had about writing poetry, ideas I had gotten from writing my own poems and from reading those of others, especially modern French poets. I told my students to write poems about their dreams, to be influenced by Williams or Stevens or Donne, to write sestinas, to collaborate on poems with each other. These things had been good for me, and some were good for some of my students. I teach now at Columbia.

My teaching of writing led me, in the late sixties, to a rather surprising new interest: teaching schoolchildren to write poetry. I taught poetry writing at P.S. 61 in New York City. I wrote a book about it, and then another book. I was lucky to have, at this time, when there was a good deal of interest in and support for educational experiment, both experience in teaching writing and an idea of poetry that made it possible for me to make it pleasant and exciting for children to write: no rhyme, no meter, be wild, be crazy, say whatever comes into your head, let the words carry you along. Later, with Kate Farrell, I taught poetry writing to old and ill people in a nursing home and wrote a book about that.

Writers, once they have survived for a while, are sometimes asked to give advice to others who write or want to. For me it has always been a good idea to read a lot and be influenced by what I read, to write a lot and try writing in different ways, to find ways of revising that are as inspiring as writing first versions, to have a few friends I can talk to, show my work to, be criticized and inspired by. It was good, also, to know another language (French poetry and France in general I found inspiring) and to be in New York. Other writers have other lives, and there is obviously a limit to what one can say about what a writer should or should not do. I wrote *Ko, or A Season on Earth*, a long (hundred-page) narrative poem, in Florence. I was supposed to be working on my doctoral dissertation. Every morning I would open my desk and look at my scholarly notes, then close the drawer and write. Someone to whom I told this (a psychiatrist) said, "There must be a more efficient way to write." I agreed, but that was the way I wrote my poem and I think the only way I could have—at least then, in 1957.

Kenneth Koch

Editor's Note:

Kenneth Koch's introduction shows the importance in a writer's career of work, resourcefulness, and a closeness to other artists. *The New York Writer's Source Book,* of course cannot be a substitute for all of this, but it can show the way for a writer to take advantage of the available sources with minimum distraction from his or her real work.

PART I: WRITERS' ORGANIZATIONS

1. PROFESSIONAL AND SERVICE ORGANIZATIONS

The Academy of American Poets

Alliance of Literary Organizations

American Society of Journalists and Authors

Center for Book Arts

Coordinating Council of Literary Magazines

The Fiction Collective

New Wilderness Foundation

New York City Department of Cultural Affairs

PEN American Center

The Poetry Center of the 92nd Street Y

The Poetry Project, St. Mark's Church in-the-Bowery

Poetry Society of America

Poets & Writers, Inc.

The Print Center, Inc.

Publishing Center for Cultural Resources

Society of Authors' Representatives

Theatre Communications Group

The Translation Center

Visual Studies Workshop

In this section we have included profiles of organizations that offer valuable services and programs to the writer, poet, playwright, and translator. Several of the organizations offer printing and publishing assistance, as do the Center for Book Arts, Publishing Center for Cultural Resources, and the Visual Studies Workshop. Organizations such as the Coordinating Council of Literary Magazines offer information on grants and other assistance to noncommercial literary magazines. And some of these organizations offer funding to writers through grants and awards.

It is important to keep in mind that other organizations profiled throughout the book offer similar services. Refer to the subject indexes for specific references.

THE ACADEMY OF AMERICAN POETS
177 East 87th Street
New York, NY 10028
(212) 427-5665

The Academy of American Poets, now in its forty-eighth year, is a nonprofit organization devoted to American poets and poetry. Its activities include sponsoring readings at the Guggenheim Museum and Donnell Library Center of the New York Public Library; awarding an annual fellowship of $10,000; sponsoring the Walt Whitman Award, the Lamont Poetry Selection, and the Harold Morton Landon Translation Prize; and awarding university and college prizes to students across the country.

Prizes and Awards

An annual fellowship award has regularly been given to American poets "for distinguished poetic achievement." Twelve chancellors, themselves eminent poets and critics, choose the poets to be so honored. Each fellow receives $10,000.

The Lamont Poetry Selection supports the publication of an American poet's second volume of poetry. Publishers are invited to submit manuscripts by once-published poets to the Academy. The winning manuscript is published as the Lamont Poetry Selection, and the winning author receives $1,000; the Academy purchases 1,200 copies of the book and distributes them to members and friends.

The Walt Whitman Award, a competition open to American citizens who have not yet published a book of poems in a standard edition, is judged and awarded to the winner by a single poet. The winning manuscript is published by a major publisher, and the author receives $1,000.

The Harold Morton Landon Translation Award, a prize of $1,000, is given to an American poet for a published translation of poetry from any language into English. An eminent poet and translator chooses the winning book.

Through special gifts, the Academy has established in the years since 1954 annual $100 poetry prizes at more than 100 colleges and universities throughout the United States. The prize programs are locally administered by the institutions at which they are offered.

Poetry Readings

The "Ten Poetry Readings" series has been given annually since 1963. Young poets, older poets of distinguished reputation, and eminent foreign poets are presented to New York audiences at the Guggenheim Museum and the Donnell Library Center. Grants from the New York City Department of Cultural Affairs have supported summer readings, bilingual programs, and children's events in city parks and branch libraries.

Workshops and Classes

The Academy has recently sponsored poetry workshops for children and teenagers in midtown Manhattan, the South Bronx, and Queens. It has also sponsored classes for high school teachers of English at branch colleges of the City University of New York.

Publications

Contributors to the Academy of $10 or more receive a monthly bulletin, *Poetry Pilot*. Each issue contains news of Academy activities and other literary events, as well as a poetry contest and a selection of poems, with commentary, by a distinguished poet. Twice a year, as a special supplement to *Poetry Pilot*, the Academy distributes a comprehensive listing of newly published books of poetry and other books by and about poets.

Fees

With payment of $30 or more as an annual fee, a member receives the monthly bulletin, *Poetry Pilot*, and a copy of the Lamont Poetry selection and the Walt Whitman Award book.

ALLIANCE OF LITERARY ORGANIZATIONS
c/o The Writers Community
120 East 89th Street
New York, NY 10028
(212) 348-0160

The purpose of the Alliance of Literary Organizations (ALO) is to encourage, foster, and promote the mutual exchange of information, knowledge, and resources among literary organizations. The ALO serves as a clearinghouse through which such organizations may apply for help or information and conducts seminars about the application of management techniques to literary organizations. The aim of the ALO is to raise the visibility of literary organizations in the nonprofit sector.

The ALO is a loose amalgamation of forty-five organizations and individuals. There are no dues, and membership simply means being on the ALO mailing list. Participating organizations represent the genres of fiction, poetry, drama, and nonfiction.

The Alliance conducts a number of seminars on management and fund raising to which members are invited. Future projects are discussed at the monthly membership meetings.

Publications

Members are kept informed of the Alliance's activities through correspondence, which includes the minutes of monthly meetings.

Fees

There are no membership fees.

AMERICAN SOCIETY OF JOURNALISTS AND AUTHORS
1501 Broadway, Suite 1907
New York, NY 10036
(212) 997-0947

The American Society of Journalists and Authors (ASJA) is a nationwide organization of independent nonfiction writers. More than 650 leading freelance writers of magazine articles, trade books, and other nonfiction writing belong to the Society. As a nonprofit literary and educational organization, the ASJA is concerned with promoting high standards of nonfiction writing. It furthers this goal through the exchange of information among working writers, monthly meetings, an annual writers' conference, the recognition of outstanding accomplishments in the field, and ongoing examinations of events and trends affecting the production and dissemination of information to the reading public.

In order to be eligible for membership, writers need to have published at least eight freelance nonfiction articles in publications of a general circulation; or two nonfiction books; or a combination of books and articles in the three years prior to application.

The ASJA offers extensive benefits and services to its members, including an exclusive referral service, confidential market information, regular meetings with editors and others in the field, group health insurance, a variety of discount services, and, above all, the opportunity to explore professional issues and concerns with other writer members. To editors and others, the ASJA offers ready access to a pool of skilled professionals who are capable of producing articles, books, brochures, and scripts on any subject.

Dial-A-Writer and Membership Directory. The ASJA matches its writers with public and private institutions through its Dial-A-Writer Service. Through this service, writers who specialize in a certain field, such as medicine, agriculture, or television, are assigned to employers. The membership directory serves a similar purpose and is sold to institutions and corporations throughout the country.

The ASJA Annual Nonfiction Writers' Conference, held each spring, is cosponsored by an institution of higher learning. The subjects of these conferences center on marketing trends. There are also regional conferences sponsored by regional chapters.

Financial Assistance

The ASJA provides financial assistance to incapacitated writers, who do not have to be members.

Publications

ASJA Newsletter. There are two sections to this monthly newsletter: one is available to nonmembers whose names are on the mailing list; the other is confidential and available to members only, since it contains marketing information. The first section is largely devoted to coverage of ASJA's conferences and panels and to news of its membership.

Books (Available directly from publishers). The ASJA has produced several books since 1954. Volumes that are currently in print are *How to Make Money Writing Magazine Articles* (edited by Beatrice Schapper, 1974; Arco Publishing Co., Inc., 219 Park Ave. South, New York, NY 10003; $5) and *A Treasury of Tips for Writers* (edited by Marvin Weisbord, revised edition, 1981; Writer's Digest Books, 9933 Alliance Road, Cincinnatti, OH 45242, $6.95, paperback).

Fees

$75 annual membership dues; initiation fee of $50.

CENTER FOR BOOK ARTS
15 Bleecker Street
New York, NY 10012
(212) 460-9768

The Center for Book Arts is a nonprofit international organization. Since 1974 the Center has promoted the arts of the book through educational programs, exhibitions, and publications. The Center runs a complete hand bindery and letterpress print shop, with limited facility for hand papermaking. The bindery and print shop take on jobs from portfolios and small editions through rebinding and artists' projects.

The staff is willing to discuss projects with writers, and give estimates on printing costs for small magazines or books, all by appointment only. The Center's facilities are also available for rental by qualified craftspeople at either an hourly or a monthly rate.

Classes

Courses are held in bookmaking techniques such as binding, both introductory and advanced, papermaking, and letterpress printing. The fees for these classes range from $125 to $175.

Weekend Workshops

In addition to its semester-long courses, the Center also conducts workshops on weekends, primarily on technique. Enrollment is limited, and fees range from $10 to $75, including the costs of materials. Subjects include letterpress technique, papermaking, binding, and the administrative and business aspects of small-press publishing.

Publications

Book Arts Review is sent free of charge to members five times a year. This publication includes feature articles on all aspects of the bookmaking craft, including small-press publishing, restoration, and supply sources. The review also prints interviews and reviews. In every issue the Book Arts Calendar lists exhibitions, lectures, classes, and readings sponsored by the Center and other organizations across the country.

Membership

Application for membership is necessary and requires supporting materials for review by the Center's executive committee. These materials should include five slides of work as well as three samples of the applicant's book craft, the former kept in the Center's files and the latter returned after review.

Fees

Student, $10; Associate, $20; Supporting, $50; Corporate, $250; Artist, $10.

"Come to the Center for Book Arts and take a few classes. Get better acquainted with production and become more involved with the book art process," encourages the Center's staff.

COORDINATING COUNCIL OF LITERARY MAGAZINES
2 Park Avenue
New York, NY 10016
(212) 481-5245

The Coordinating Council of Literary Magazines (CCLM) is a national, nonprofit literary organization that provides grants and services to noncommercial literary magazines. It sponsors an annual meeting of editors and writers and provides other resources and services to editors, writers, and readers of literature.

Grants and Awards

Grants to Literary Magazines

Any noncommercial literary magazine (tax-exempt status not required) that has been in operation for at least one year and has published a minimum of three issues may apply for CCLM grants. These grants may be used for general support of publication, authors' payments, and special needs. Grants range from $500 to $3,500.

Deadlines are usually in early September and late January. Grants committees composed of editors and writers meet in the fall and spring of each year to review grant proposals. In order to ensure impartiality, grants committees of five individuals serve for one season only; three members are elected by CCLM membership and two are appointed by the board of directors, who give final approval for all grants.

Special Assistance Grants (Seed Money)

For the purpose of serving ethnic groups, minorities, and isolated regions, a limited number of special grants are given to new magazines that have published fewer than three issues.

College Contests

In a competition for undergraduate literary magazines, six prizes are offered each year: one first prize of $500, two second prizes of $200, and three third prizes of $100.

To be entered in the competition, magazines must publish primarily creative writing, the contributors must be at least 50 percent undergraduate students, and they must be edited by undergraduates.

Decisions, announced in the fall, are based on the quality of writing, editorial work, and graphic design.

Library

Consisting of 12,000 volumes of 1,500 magazines acquired since 1967, this library is available for use by the general public by appointment. No volumes may be taken out. The hours of the library are 10:00–12:00 and 2:30–4:30, Monday through Friday.

Internship Programs

CCLM internships are available in the categories of editing, publicity, and library work. Some of these are salaried by the Urban Corps/Federal College Work-Study Program.

Regional Meetings

Regional conferences for editors and writers are held twice a year, in the spring and the fall. Meetings last from two to three days, and readings, panels, and workshops are held on both the technical and editorial aspects of publishing as well as topics of literary interest. Business and grants committee meetings are also held at this time.

Fiscal Agent

CCLM acts as a fiscal agent for its membership magazines that do not have 501(c) 3 (tax-exempt) status.

Publications

CCLM Newsletter is published four times a year; the newsletter reports on funding developments, requests for manuscripts, information on contests, grant and prize deadlines, workshops, conferences, and services across the United States. The annual subscription, as of 1983, is $5.

Catalog of Literary Magazines (published annually, $4.95) includes descriptive entries for over 340 literary magazines.

Catalog of College Literary Magazines (published annually, $2) includes entries for 200 college literary magazines.

A Guide to Organizing and Exhibiting at Book Fairs ($2) is available from CCLM; all orders must be prepaid.

Fees

Membership dues are $10 a year.

THE FICTION COLLECTIVE
c/o Department of English
Brooklyn College, Brooklyn, NY 11210
(212) 780-5480

The Fiction Collective is a publishing collective devoted to fiction. Membership is based on the Collective's acceptance for publication of a submitted manuscript. Writers share in the editing, costs, and other duties of running a small, not-for-profit publishing firm. Although some grants are given to help defray costs, the potential author is generally expected to provide half of the amount of production costs for the book, which is then returned to him or her from the revenue of book sales.

The Fiction Collective has published more than thirty titles so far; most were novels, and two were anthologies. Writers who have published titles through the Collective include Walter Abish, Russell Banks, Jerry Bumpus, Robert Coover, Raymond Federman, Ursule Molinaro, and Ronald Sukenick.

Student interns work at the Collective each year, helping to run the office and providing editorial assistance. These internships are salaried by the Urban Corps/Federal College Work-Study Program and were developed by the Arts Apprenticeship Program (see separate listing).

Readings are arranged for Fiction Collective writers at libraries, bookstores, and colleges.

Publications

To order the *Annual Catalogue of Publications*, write to the Fiction Collective.

NEW WILDERNESS FOUNDATION
325 Spring Street, Room 208
New York, NY 10013
(212) 807-7944

The New Wilderness Foundation is a nonprofit artists' collective that creates connections between traditional and contemporary arts through cross-ethnic music, poetry, mixed media, and collaborative performances. Its Ocarina Orchestra and Wind Band, which follow the tradition of earlier community musicians, are devoted to collective, improvised music making. The Foundation produces two annual multimedia events, presented outdoors and offered free to the public: a Summer Solstice Celebration in June and the International Radio Solstice, the Great Wind Event, in October.

New Wilderness maintains an Artist Access Sound Studio that offers artists postproduction studio time, equipment, audio engineering facilities, and assistance at low rates. By appointment: (212) 724-8118.

Cassette tape archives of music, sound, and poetry of international and interethnic sources are accessible to the public in the studio's Listening Room. By appointment: (212) 807-7944. (See profile in Chapter 12.)

Opportunities to give readings are offered at the Great Wind Event and in conjunction with the reading series held at the Ear Inn at 326 Spring Street.

Internship Programs

Training positions in editorial work and publishing are offered by the Foundation's two publications: the *New Wilderness Letter* and *EAR Magazine East*.

The Artist Access Sound Studio offers internships to students studying recording production, audio engineering, and other related fields. These internships are for students who are eligible for Urban Corps/Federal College Work-Study grants (see Department of Cultural Affairs/Arts Apprenticeship entry).

Production training is also available during the academic year through the International Radio Solstice and other radio projects relating to experimental music, sound, and performance.

Publications

New Wilderness publications connect readers and listeners with contemporary and experimental musicians, poets, performers, and visual artists.

EAR Magazine East, a subscription tabloid published five times a year, is devoted to source material and original sound texts of innovative phonetic, electronic, and gesture performances of music and sound poetry. Annual subscription: $12; single copies: $1.50.

New Wilderness Letter is a literary magazine/book published twice a year which emphasizes new techniques of prosody, poetics, performance poetry, rituals, dance, and the analysis of these. Annual subscription: $7; single copies: $3.50.

New Wilderness Audiographics is an ongoing series of cassette tapes featuring new, ancient, and ethnic explorations in music, song, chanting, poetry, drama, and storytelling. Write for a current listing.

Fees

There is no membership fee.

> "In this age of technological communication, the writer must give much thought to his or her vehicle for expression. Your audience may be in a small circle of weekly readings or an international circle of radio/TV enthusiasts."
> —Statement from New Wilderness

NEW YORK CITY DEPARTMENT OF CULTURAL AFFAIRS
2 Columbus Circle
New York, NY 10019

The New York City Department of Cultural Affairs was established in 1976 to consolidate and extend New York City's long-standing commitment to the arts. The agency's mandate, as specified in the City Charter, is "to plan, develop, conduct and supervise cultural activities and facilities" and to "foster coordination among city, state, and federal agencies, other organizations and institutions with respect to cultural activities in the city."

The Department administers direct city support for operating expenses and capital planning and improvements at thirty cultural institutions located primarily in city-owned facilities. The city is now in partnership with a diverse group of institutions, including the Metropolitan Museum of Art, the Museum of Natural History, the Queens Museum, the Bronx Zoo, El Museo del Barrio, and the Staten Island Historical Society.

The Department also contributes to free or low-cost cultural activities in parks, schools, community centers, and public facilities citywide. For example, the city enters into contracts with the Metropolitan Opera and the New York Philharmonic for concerts that draw several hundred thousands to the city's parks each summer.

Of particular relevance to writers is the Arts Apprenticeship Program, which was created by the New York City Department of Cultural Affairs in 1974 to develop apprenticeships/internships for university students interested in careers in the arts and literature. The program houses a resource center that provides descriptions of apprenticeships with more than three hundred service organizations and individual writers and artists.

Students in colleges and universities who are eligible for work-study may receive salaries by arranging eligibility with their college financial aid offices (see Urban Corps profile). Those not eligible for work-study can work as volunteers or can arrange to receive academic credit through agreements with their schools or universities.

The Arts Apprenticeship Program also maintains current career information for writers on file. In addition to this guide, the Arts Apprenticeship Program has prepared a source book for visual artists.

PEN AMERICAN CENTER
47 Fifth Avenue
New York, NY 10003
(212) 255-1977

PEN American Center is one of eighty centers of PEN International, the only world association of literary writers. The Center was established to promote international understanding, fellowship, and cooperation among writers of the world. American PEN's activities include panel discussions, receptions for authors, conferences, international congresses, and assistance to writers in prison and to writers with immediate financial needs.

Membership is open to writers of poetry, fiction, translation, essays, plays, and to editors who have published two or more books of literary merit in the United States.

PEN's Committees

PEN is comprised of several committees designed to address different situations of writers in America and abroad. These committees produce publications of their research.

"Freedom to Write" lobbies against the harassment of writers in the United States and around the world; it sponsors programs concerning international issues. "The Publishing Industry Committee" is concerned largely with the conglomerate trend in the publishing industry and what it means for authors. The "Translation Committee" promotes the art of literary translation, giving awards for new work, and disseminates information on translators' contracts and standard fees. These committees produce reports on their findings, which are covered in the newsletter.

The programs noted below may be of particular interest to non-members as well as members.

PEN Writers Fund

PEN provides emergency grants not exceeding $500 to writers in case of illness, medical expenses, unemployment, or any other situation deemed by PEN members as constituting an emergency. (For information about emergency funds, see Change, Inc., a similar program set up for writers as well as artists.) Recipients of the PEN grant must be New York State residents and should be prepared to demonstrate their professional status to the committee. Once the application has been approved by the committee, funds are dispatched promptly, sometimes within twenty-four hours.

Prison Writing Program

This program promotes and encourages creative writing among prisoners in New York State, administers an annual contest, and provides information and referrals to inmates about writing and publishing. It is also developing a library program for New York State prisons.

Prizes and Awards

For Translation

PEN awards prizes for translation from works in Italian, Portuguese, German, and the Scandinavian languages into English. With the exception of the Italian award of $3,000, each of these awards is $500. In addition to the awards for specific languages, PEN awards a prize of $1,000 for any distinguished book-length translation.

For New American Writers

Ernest Hemingway Foundation Award. $6,000 for the best first-published work of fiction by an American writer.

PEN Writing Award for Prisoners. $525 for the best work by a prison writer.

For Distinguished Fiction. The PEN/Faulkner Award for fiction is given annually to an author for the finest work of fiction published that year.

For Editors. PEN Publishers Citation and Lucille J. Medwick Award. The former is given for service in international letters; the latter is given to a publisher and an editor who has served the cause of young, unrecognized, and promising writers.

Readings, Panels, and Symposia

Readings are given of works in progress by PEN members, and there is also a series of readings by writers given twice yearly in which new and unpublished writers of merit are introduced to the community.

Panels and symposia are given on issues of interest to writers and editors, such as "Book Publishing in the 80s," "Writers and Convicts: An American Romance," and "Vietnam Voices: The War in American Literature."

Internship Program

PEN regularly offers internships (through colleges and the Urban Corps) to undergraduate and graduate students who demonstrate an interest in writing and literature.

Publications

PEN Standards (#1) for Magazine and Periodical Assignments. Recommended procedures as the basis for all working arrangements between writers and magazine editors. Free.

PEN Standards (#2) for Author's Access to Information from Book Publishers. Guidelines to help authors obtain information about works under contract, which is not readily made available by publishers. Free.

A Translator's Model Contract (includes the rights of the translator). Recommendations for translators on rates, assignments, contracts, and other matters. Free.

Prison Writing Information Bulletin #6. Advice and information for incarcerated writers on writing and publishing, market listings, and lists of service organizations for prisoners. Free.

In Preparation: The Right to Translate. A new position paper for translators on the legal and ethical problems of the translator. Free.

(Newsletter subscribers who are not PEN members may also receive notification about PEN events—readings, symposia, conferences—by subscription. $15 membership fee includes newsletter.)

Grants and Awards Available to American Writers, 12th edition, 1982–83. PEN American Center, 47 Fifth Avenue, New York, NY 10003. $5 to individuals, $8.50 to libraries and institutions. This new edition lists nearly 500 American and international grants programs for all kinds of writers: grants for poets and novelists, fellowships for scholars and researchers, production opportunities for playwrights and radio and screenwriters. Gives guidelines, deadlines, and summaries of application procedures. Includes an appendix of American and Canadian state arts councils and indexes of grants according to discipline.

Un-American Activities: The Campaign Against the Underground Press. By Geoffrey Rips. A report on the illegal surveillance and harassment of the independent press movement of the 1960s and 1970s. $7.95, paperback.

The World of Translation. Second printing, 1981. A collection of essays on the art of literary translation. $8.95, paperback.

PENewsletter. Published quarterly, the newsletter reports on issues vital to the literary community, covers PEN's activities in the United States and abroad, and features interviews and reminiscences by international literary figures. Subscription is $5 yearly, $1.25 for a sample issue.

Fees

Annual membership dues are $35.

> "It has been said that good writers are a national resource, like green trees and clear water, and that if they need help they should not go unaided."
> —Statement from Pen Writer's Fund

THE POETRY CENTER OF THE 92nd STREET Y
1395 Lexington Avenue
New York, NY 10028
(212) 427-6000

Founded in 1939 as a membership organization, the Poetry Center schedules roughly fifty writers each year to read their works. There is also a series of lectures and seminars; and writing workshops are conducted at the Dalton School during the academic year.

In the past, participants in the Center's activities have included Robert Frost, T. S. Eliot, and Wallace Stevens. Presentations, however, are not restricted to poetry. The 1982 reading and lecture series included playwrights Tennessee Williams and Sam Shephard and novelists D. M. Thomas and William Styron.

Awards

"Discovery"/The Nation Contest. As of 1983, this contest was in its eighth year. Its aim is to bring attention to poets who have never published a book. The four winners selected each year are awarded a reading at the "Y" and publication in *The Nation*. Deadlines are usually at the beginning of the year. For specifics on deadlines and length of entries, contact the Poetry Center office at 427-6000, extension 176.

Educational Programs and Workshops

Writers in Residence. The Center hosts a resident who teaches both at the Poetry Center and in selected high schools in New York City.

Workshops. Each year there are six workshops in poetry, one in play writing, one in fiction, and one in criticism and reviewing. Workshop members are chosen by individual instructors through review of submitted manuscripts. The Center reserves the right to restrict the number of workshops an individual may take at one time. Sessions open in September and in January. Call for application requirements.

Buttenweiser Library of the Center maintains a literary collection of writers who appear at the Poetry Center. It houses, as well, a selection of literary journals and periodicals. Library privileges are restricted to members and to workshop participants only during the term in which they are enrolled.

Fees

Tuition for workshops ranges from $135 to $165.

Membership benefits include free admission to all readings, reductions on prices for special events, reduced-rate parking, and discounts at neighborhood restaurants. One year, $50; Patron, $150; Benefactor, $300.

THE POETRY PROJECT
St. Mark's Church in-the-Bowery
2nd Avenue and 10th Street
New York, NY 10003
(212) 674-0910

Founded in 1966 at the St. Mark's Church, the Poetry Project is one of the largest and most dynamic poetry centers in the country. Although it began as an outgrowth of the small-press movement in New York during the late 1950s and 1960s, it now has an international scope, while still maintaining its roots in the neighborhood of the Lower East Side. The Poetry Project champions the oral tradition, sponsors free workshops, and makes poetry accessible in an experimental atmosphere. There is a regular schedule of readings, free workshops, and lectures.

There are two weekly reading series: Monday nights are devoted to Poetry/Performance, and on Wednesday nights there are readings, and in the spring, workshop readings are offered. Open readings are held the first Monday of every month (see Poetry Project Tape Collection, page 170). There are between one and three free, open, and ongoing writing workshops per week, plus occasional short residencies from out-of-town poets.

Publications

The Poetry Project publishes the *Poetry Project Newsletter* and various workshop magazines. Inquire for further details.

Fees

Membership fees range from $25 to $300 per year and offer free admission to most programs, readings, performances, lectures, and free copies of publications and records.

POETRY SOCIETY OF AMERICA
15 Gramercy Park
New York, NY 10003
(212) 254-9628
254-9683

The Poetry Society of America, founded in 1910, is a nonprofit membership organization dedicated to the promotion of poetry and poets. Each year it awards prizes in amounts of up to $10,000. It sponsors readings and lectures in conjunction with the Poetics Institute of New York University, and poetry workshops are held in the fall and spring at the PSA offices at 15 Gramercy Park. In addition to publishing a bulletin and newsletter, the PSA oversees a book distribution program, whereby remaindered books of poetry are distributed to prisons and nursing homes throughout the country.

Members are elected on the basis of either the work they submit or their reputation as poets; associate membership is open to teachers, critics, and scholars. Write PSA for application and procedures.

Monthly Reading Series. Poets are invited by the Governing Board Program Committee to read. This series is cosponsored by the Poetics Institute.

Spotlight Reading Series. This series provides PSA members who are unpublished with the opportunity to read their work and to gain exposure in the community.

Workshops. These are held at PSA offices. For more information, call 254-9628.

Award Series. About eighteen different cash awards, ranging from $100 to $2,425, are presented by the PSA each year. Recipients include students and established writers. Announcements are made at the PSA annual awards ceremony.

Library. The Van Voorhis Poetry Library has more than 6,000 volumes, including books of poetry, biography, commentary, and a permanent audio-tape collection. The library is open to the public.

Advisory Services. Both members and nonmembers may obtain from Society headquarters free information about contests, publications, poetry resources, other members in their areas, and workshops and readings.

Publications

PSA Bulletin. Published four times a year. Features excerpts from PSA programs and the work of poets and critics.

PSA Newsletter. Published three times a year. Features membership news.

Fees

The fee when accepted as a member is $20.

POETS & WRITERS, INC.
201 West 54th Street
New York, NY 10019
(212) 757-1766

Poets & Writers serves as an extensive information center and service organization for literary activities nationwide, and it supports and sponsors readings and workshops in New York State.

Information Center

Their Information Center may be contacted by telephone from 11:00 A.M. to 3:00 P.M. Eastern Time, Monday through Friday. Poets & Writers offers help, information, and advice to writers on general professional questions such as grant eligibility, copywrighting, and submissions to magazines. Up-to-date files are kept on 5,400 poets and fiction writers whose work has been published in the United States. The addresses and individual data for all these writers are available to anyone by phone or by mail as well as through the annual directories published by the Center.

Financial Assistance

In New York State, Poets & Writers supplements fees paid to writers for readings and workshops. Organizations that sponsor literary events and apply to P & W for financial assistance include libraries, Y's, community centers, arts groups, universities, museums, writers' groups, neighborhood houses, religious organizations, and bookstores. P & W helps more than 300 sponsors each year, and in 1981 supplemental fees that ranged from $75 to $300 were given to 486 writers.

Publications

Coda, the P & W newsletter, is published five times a year. It covers awards, prizes, and publishing opportunities and contains articles that address professional questions such as small-press publishing, manuscript submission, alternative careers, and so on. Reprints of *Coda* articles are available for $1 each. Subjects of the articles also include writers' colonies, resources, jobs, public readings, and taxes.

Directory of American Poets and Fiction Writers, 1980–81 edition, includes names, addresses, and telephone numbers of 4,852 poets and fiction writers published in the United States. Information is included on each writer's publications, spoken languages, work preference, and minority affiliation. $10, paperback; $14.50, hardcover.

Literary Bookstores: A List in Progress ($2.50). A list of 344 stores that specialize in contemporary fiction and poetry with notes on such biases as bilingualism or feminism and an appendix listing thirty-four literary bars and coffee houses.

Literary Agents: A Complete Guide ($3.95). This booklet is directed at poets and novelists interested in publishing. It is a useful introduction to the different types of agents, their functions, and how to find one. It includes a list of forty-four agents who accept unsolicited manuscripts and a list of five other resources for finding agents.

Sponsors List ($3.50). This includes 606 organizations across the nation that sponsor readings and workshops involving poets and fiction writers.

A Writer's Guide to Copyright ($4.95). A simply written summary of the 1979 copyright law for writers, editors, and teachers.

Free Brochures—"How to Organize a Reading or Workshop" and "How to Publicize Readings and Workshops"—are available from Poets & Writers. To receive the titles, send a self-addressed stamped envelope.

Poets & Writers also rents a mailing list of its members—individuals, libraries, and organizations interested in contemporary poetry and fiction. This list is updated five times a year and all addresses are current. Call or write to Department ML to order the list.

THE PRINT CENTER, INC.
Box 1050
Brooklyn, NY 11202
(212) 875-4482

Founded in 1971 as a nonprofit organization, the Print Center provides a full range of printing and production services to noncommercial publishers of literature, the arts, and other work in the public interest. Services are also available to individual writers and artists.

In addition to small-press books and magazines, the Print Center produces flyers, posters, pamphlets, and postcards, usually at prices that are significantly lower than commercial rates. The staff consists of people who are both printing pros and experienced writers, artists, and editors.

Estimate of Printing Costs

Anyone working on a publication may receive an estimate of printing costs by filling out the back of the Print Center's publicity card. Inquire at the address above.

Services to Customers

Typesetting, design and layout, camera work, proofreading, printing, and binding are the services that the Print Center provides.

Workshops

Workshops on various aspects of printing and design are held from time to time. Customers may also do some of their own work as a learning experience and to effect further savings.

Publications

"How to Prepare Your Publication for the Press." Free upon request with self-addressed stamped envelope.

PUBLISHING CENTER FOR CULTURAL RESOURCES
625 Broadway
New York, NY 10012
(212) 260-2010

The Publishing Center is a nonprofit organization that exists exclusively to help nonprofit groups and institutions produce well-planned, realistically budgeted publications. It came into being in 1973 in response to needs recognized by the New York State Council on the Arts—specifically the need for competent publishing personnel in most arts institutions. The Center's services are largely arts related and centered in New York State. Museums, historical societies, performance groups, environmentalists, service organizations, government agencies, and art organizations use the Publishing Center's resources.

The Center provides four major services:

Planning assesses the size, needs, and resources of a publication. The Center helps to tailor the format and production process, prepares cost estimates, and offers technical assistance.

Production service includes the reading and editing of manuscripts, the preparation of artwork, and professional printing.

Cooperative printing assembles print runs of postcards, notes, and posters. Individual artists can take advantage of this service by obtaining sponsorship from a nonprofit organization.

Distribution takes books on consignment, fills orders, accepts payment, accounts for inventory and receipts, and remits quarterly to the publishing body. All titles distributed are advertised in *Publishers' Trade List Annual*, which enables researchers throughout the country to learn of their existence and how to order them.

Free estimates are given, but costs are involved in some of the Publishing Center's services. Planning services are available free of charge to any nonprofit organization. Write or telephone to inquire about how any of the Print Center's services can best assist specific publication projects.

SOCIETY OF AUTHORS' REPRESENTATIVES
P.O. Box 650
Old Chelsea Station
New York, NY 10113
(212) 741-1356

The Society of Authors' Representatives (SAR) is a professional organization of literary and dramatic agents. This is a voluntary association of agents whose individual members subscribe to prescribed ethical practices as authors' business representatives. The Society does not offer or recommend agents to writers; however, it regularly publishes a list of member agents who handle both dramatic and literary clients.

Publication

"The Literary Agent" is a brochure that lists SAR agents and outlines the steps necessary to obtain an agent. It also describes standard practices of agents as well as what an agent does or does not do. This pamphlet is free with a self-addressed, stamped envelope.

Fees

Contact SAR for eligibility requirements.

THEATRE COMMUNICATIONS GROUP

355 Lexington Avenue
New York, NY 10017
(212) 697-5230

Contact: M. Elizabeth Osborn
Literary Services Associate

The Theatre Communications Group is the national membership organization for the nonprofit professional theater. TCG offers programs and services to a constituency of nearly two hundred theaters, as well as to thousands of individual theater artists, technicians, and administrators. Altogether, programs and publications of the Literary Services department provide the most comprehensive cooperative system in existence to encourage and support the creation, development, and production of new works for the American theater. The Literary Services department provides a clearinghouse and acts as liaison among playwrights, translators, composers, librettists, lyricists, directors, and literary managers—in short, everyone involved in creating and producing new works for the stage.

Programs are designed to extend the lines of communication through which new material and its authors become known and presented; to expand the awareness of theaters, educational institutions, and other concerned organizations and individuals about contemporary work; to provide informational and advisory assistance to writers and composers; to maintain a forum for the discussion of issues important to those who create new works for the stage, enabling the department to function as an "ombudsman" for writers, composers, and literary managers in the noncommercial theater.

Publications

Theatre Communications is an illustrated monthly publication that includes a regular column, "Plays and Playwrights," with information on competition deadlines.

Dramatists Sourcebook: This unique, definitive guide is for playwrights, translators, composers, lyricists, and librettists seeking to work in the nonprofit professional theater. Revised annually, it includes comprehensive listings of fellowships, grants, contests, awards, service organizations, useful publications, artist colonies, and state arts council programs.

Plays in Process: TCG's national script-circulation service distributes at least twelve new scripts annually. Chosen by a selection committee of distinguished theater professionals, each script must have

41

received a full production at one of TCG's constituent nonprofit professional theaters during the season in which it is distributed to subscribers. Subscribers also receive *Play Source*, an information bulletin listing other new plays.

New Plays USA 1: An anthology of plays from America's professional theaters, chosen from the *Plays in Process* script-circulation service.

Theater Profiles: A biennial illustrated reference guide to America's nonprofit professional theaters.

Theater Directory: An annual pocket-sized directory of America's professional theaters.

Many other publications are available; contact TCG for a catalog and further information.

Fees

Fees for member theaters are based on income. Individuals may avail themselves of many TCG services without charge. Playwrights would be interested in the literary services that TCG provides.

THE TRANSLATION CENTER
Mathematics Building, Room 307A
Columbia University
New York, NY 10027
(212) 280-2305

The Translation Center is dedicated to furthering excellence in the translation of literary works. The aim of the Center's program is forwarded in two ways: through financial support in the form of awards, fellowships, and subventions offered to translators and through the Center's journal, *Translation*, which encourages a broader audience for foreign literature and acts as a showcase for translators.

Conferences and seminars are conducted by foreign writers and translators concerning their art.

Publications

Translation is published semiannually. Contact the Translation Center for subscription rates.

VISUAL STUDIES WORKSHOP*
31 Prince Street
Rochester, NY 14607
(716) 442-8676   **Contact: Joan Lyons**

The Visual Studies Workshop was founded in 1969 as an international center for the study and interpretation of photography and related disciplines. Over the years the Workshop's interest has expanded to include artists' and writers' books, videotapes, and films. The VSW has had a long-standing interest in books as the primary medium of expression and, in 1972, established the VSW Press.

The VSW Press works with artists, writers, and nonprofit organizations on the production of books, catalogs, posters, and limited-edition offset prints. More than two hundred books have been produced, including artists' books, independent press poetry, and technical and critical historical anthologies concerning the visual arts. Services include typesetting and prepress production, design and production consultations, as well as workshops in book design and production. Interns and apprentices are accepted.

The Book Service maintains a bookstore at VSW, mail-order services, and a series of book exhibitions. The Research Center houses a permanent collection of prints, books, periodicals, slides, and information files relevant to the study of visual imagery. The Independent Press Archive contains a collection of 2,000 artists' books acquired through donations and acquisitions. It is catalogued and cross-referenced for research.

Publications

Afterimage, the VSW's monthly journal of photography, independent film and video, and artists' books, makes a valuable contribution to the field of independent art publishing through its book reviews. Books received for review are placed in the Independent Press Archive.

Fees

Membership in the VSW is $20 and includes a one-year subscription to *Afterimage* and a discount on all VSW books and publications.

---

*Although this organization is located in Rochester, New York, it is included in this book because it is a major center for the production of artists' books and should be of interest to many writers. It is also a good model for groups wanting to start their own production services centers.

2. GUILDS AND ADVOCACY GROUPS

Authors Guild, Inc., and the Authors League of America, Inc.

The Dramatists Guild, Inc.

The National Association of Third World Writers

National Writers Union

New York Area Media Alliance

Volunteer Lawyers for the Arts

Writers Guild of America, East, Inc.

The rationale for unifying these organizations into a chapter is that each concentrates on collective advocacy for its members' professional interests as its primary function. The chapters assist their members with such legal questions as contract terms and rights and copyright; in addition, many offer health benefits. Some of them bring members together for seminars and conferences where issues relevant to writers are discussed.

AUTHORS GUILD, INC., AND
THE AUTHORS LEAGUE OF AMERICA, INC.
234 West 44th Street
New York, NY 10036
(212) 398-0838

These two closely related membership organizations, the Authors Guild, Inc., founded in 1921, and the Authors League of America, Inc., founded in 1912, are open only to the established professional. Membership in the League qualifies one for membership in the Guild. Members are required to show publishing credentials, either with magazines of a substantial circulation or with an established American publisher. Some recent and current members reflect the prestige of the League and the Guild: John Updike, Art Buchwald, Arthur Schlesinger, Jr., and the late John Cheever. Membership includes writers of fiction, nonfiction, and poetry.

To meet eligibility requirements the author must have written a book published by an established company at least seven years prior to application, or three or more magazine pieces published eighteen months prior to application; or have such professional standing, in the opinion of the membership committee, that he or she shall be entitled to membership.

The Dramatists Guild, Inc., is affiliated with the Authors League and Guild, and members of the DG are automatically qualified for membership in both affiliates.

Matters of joint concern to authors and dramatists, such as copyright and freedom of expression, remain in the province of the League; other matters, such as contract terms and subsidiary rights, are in the province of the Authors and Dramatists Guild. These organizations regard their predominant role as collective advocates for their members' professional interests. The support provided includes:

Symposia, in which experts discuss matters of professional interest to writers.

Advice and assistance to members on professional and business problems. Limitations on this function are imposed by the number of facilities and staff available.

Publications

Authors Guild Bulletin. This publication is distributed to members every two months. The bulletin includes detailed articles on professional questions, such as copyright litigation, censorship, taxation, marketing trends, and interviewing techniques.

Fees

There is no initiation fee. The annual dues for Authors Guild active members are $50. A new member pays $50 when he joins, payable within sixty days. Dues for subsequent years may be paid either annually or in two semiannual installments. Professional writers can deduct dues as an expense on income tax returns.

THE DRAMATISTS GUILD, INC.
234 West 44th Street
New York, NY 10036
(212) 398-9366

"The Dramatists Guild is the only professional association of play-wrights, composers, and lyricists in the United States today," states the Guild. All theater writers are eligible for active or associate membership; other people interested in the Guild may become subscribing members. The Guild's services are offered to more than 6,000 members across the country.

The Guild was originally formed with the purpose of protecting its members' rights to copyright and artistic control of musicals and plays in the United States. Some of its earliest members were Eugene O'Neill, Cole Porter, and Oscar Hammerstein. Members of its council presently include Edward Albee, Jules Feiffer, Ira Levin, and David Mamet, to name just a few.

The Guild's services are available to its members only. These services include business and marketing advice, symposia, access to a reference library, and health insurance benefits, as well as the protection of artistic rights through its Minimum Basic Contract.

Active and associate membership entitles the writer to membership in both the Authors Guild and the Authors League of America. (See separate profiles.)

DG's publications often contain highly detailed information related to professional concerns, such as theaters willing to read unsolicited manuscripts, copyright law, and dramatic agents. A partial listing of these services is given below.

Contracts

The Guild's first and foremost service is the securing and co-signing of Minimum Basic Contracts for the dramatic and musical works of its members. These contracts guarantee that the work is not altered in any way without the author's consent and that the author get the appropriate royalties. Copies of these contracts are available for $2.00 a copy.

Business Advice

DG's executive director and legal assistant regularly give advice to

members on business matters such as options, contracts, copyrig
taxes, and dealings with producers and agents.

Marketing Information

The Guild's staff informs members of the whereabouts of producers
and agents and acts as a liaison for producers wishing to get in touch
with members. It also provides them with information on grants,
theaters, contests, workshops, conferences, and other opportunities.

Reference Library and Newsroom

The Guild's library houses members' books and plays, copies of all
Guild contracts from 1926 to the present, and standard theater reference texts. The newsroom contains more current information on
theaters, awards, grants, contests, and residencies.

Health Insurance

All members are entitled to a Blue Cross/Blue Shield health plan.

Publications

Dramatists Guild Quarterly. Available through membership only, this
quarterly contains transcripts of symposia, commentaries, letters, and
notices of productions and frequently lists information about professional opportunities. The Summer 1982 issue contains a directory of
agents, a list of regional theaters accepting manuscripts, and updates
on grants and play contests.

Dramatists Guild Newsletter. Available to members only, the
newsletter is published monthly and runs announcements submitted
by members regarding forthcoming productions, manuscript searches,
and requests for collaborators.

Fees

Active members, $35 annually; associate members, $20 annually; subscribing members, $15 annually.

Call or write the Dramatists Guild for membership-eligibility requirements.

THE NATIONAL ASSOCIATION OF THIRD WORLD WRITERS
373 Fifth Avenue Suite 1007
New York, NY 10016

The National Association of Third World Writers was organized in 1980 to discuss ways to lobby and eliminate the institutional neglect by the Literature Program of the National Endowment for the Arts in its allocation of grants to third world writers. Since September 1982, the Association has been compiling a list of publishers, presses, periodicals, bookstores, and distributors that are committed to working with the literature of third world writers. Send inquiries to Gale Jackson at the above address.

Publications

Jes' Grew is a newsletter containing information that fosters communication among third world writers across geographic and ethnic lines. It is also a resource for information about grants and application procedures.

Fees

There is a membership fee of $30 a year. Membership is open to all third world writers in the United States. Call for further information.

NATIONAL WRITERS UNION
OCNWU-NY Local
63 West 8th Street
New York, NY 10011
(212) 473-3753

The National Writers Union is still in the state of organizing, advocating, and lobbying for a national union to obtain greater rights for artists. At issue is a deep grievance about the status of writers in America. Participants of already formed organizing committees throughout the country are meeting regularly to help establish this National Writers Union. The organizers believe that the union would be able to protect writers with legal or professional pressure on issues such as nonpayment, unaccountability for payment, insensitivity to editorial suggestions, and lack of legal protection.

The National Writers Union has become a topic of concern for writers all over the country. Regional conferences are still being planned in various parts of the country. Please call the New York Local at the above number if you want to get involved in continuing this struggle for a National Writers Union.

Statement from the National Writers Union

In October 1981 the American Writers' Congress voted overwhelmingly to form a national writers union. Although many have predicted that writers are "loners" and "too individualistic to organize," successful writers unions are now functioning in several countries, including Great Britain, Denmark, Sweden, and Canada. The (screen) Writers Guild of America, for example, is one of the most successful unions in this country. Since the time of the Congress, locals of an organizing committee for a national writers union with a total of more than 1,500 members have begun to function in fifteen cities, including Washington, Boston, San Francisco, and New York.

The need for action was obvious. A recent Columbia University survey only confirmed what most writers already knew: the average author (defined as a contemporary American writer who had published at least one book) earns less than $5,000 a year from writing; that only 5 percent of authors are able to sustain themselves by writing; and only 38 percent of these earn over $20,000—the median income for an average American family.

For poets and prose writers, magazine and book authors, a successful writers union will bargain collectively with publishers, enforce contractual agreements, and launch job actions. It will establish grievance procedures and negotiate advances and minimum magazine rates based on publishers' gross assets. A comprehensive health plan will be offered and, moving into new areas of authors' rights, a union will press for extra pay for extra rewrites, for the elimination of "kill fees" or work-for-hire contracts, and for the establishment of a public-lending right to assure authors of payments every time their books are borrowed from the library.

The New York City Local, one of the first locals to get off the ground, has more than 180 members. It has passed and recommended to the national union proposals for membership, structure, a constitution and by-laws, and detailed grievance procedures. Interest and participation are growing. The publishing world is taking our union seriously. But we have a long way to go, and much work still needs to be accomplished—recruitment, strategy, research, action. Our effectiveness will depend on the membership and the support of all writers.

If you are interested in becoming a member of the New York Local or finding out more about the Organizing Committee for a National Writers Union (OCNWU), write to OCNWU-NY Local, 63 West 8th Street, New York, NY 10011 or telephone (212) 473-3753.

NEW YORK AREA MEDIA ALLIANCE
306 West 100th Street, #21
New York, NY 10025
(212) 865-7598

The Media Alliance is a group of journalists who cooperate to help each other with articles. The aim of the Alliance is to improve the quality of media coverage. The Alliance provides assistance to free-lance writers by offering health insurance and holding meetings at which writers have the opportunity to meet with editors.

The Alliance sponsors conferences, workshops, and forums with the purpose of exchanging information on professional aspects of journalism.

Workshops are held with community groups to further the cause of improving press coverage. There are forums on special subjects, such as labor reporting, the use of word processors, and other subjects of interest to professional journalists.

Members meet regularly to discuss articles on which they are working. Editors are invited to discussions with free-lancers on how to write for publication. Members must be working journalists, free-lance writers, or staff members of print or broadcast organizations.

Publications

A newsletter is published monthly and is sent to members.

Fees

$15 a year.

VOLUNTEER LAWYERS FOR THE ARTS
165 West 46th Street, Suite 711 (office)
New York, NY 10036

1560 Broadway, Suite 711 (mailing address)
New York, NY 10036
(212) 575-1150

Volunteer Lawyers for the Arts (VLA) is a nonprofit tax-exempt organization that arranges free legal representation by volunteer attorneys for artists and arts organizations unable to afford private counsel. It provides legal referral, conducts educational programs, and publishes a quarterly journal, *Art and the Law.*

Artists and arts groups who are financially eligible and who have an arts-related legal problem are referred by the VLA to one of more than five hundred volunteer attorneys. These attorneys handle a variety of problems for VLA clients, such as incorporation of nonprofit groups, securing tax exemptions, contracts, copyright, tax, labor, and other issues.

Artists' Hotline (See Foundation for the Community of Artists.) VLA attorneys are stationed at the FCA's Artists' Hotline two days every week to answer a number of legal questions.

Publications

Art and the Law is a quarterly journal at a yearly subscription rate of $20.

(For more information about pamphlets on specific issues, see bibliography.)

Fees

An administrative fee of $15 to $50 is charged. There is no fee for legal services.

WRITERS GUILD OF AMERICA, EAST, INC.
555 West 57th Street
New York, NY 10019
(212) 245-6180

The Writers Guild of America is a labor union that represents writers in motion pictures, television, and other media. It negotiates Minimum Basic Agreements with producers and major broadcasting networks for writers, thus protecting the financial interests of its members.

Its sister organization, WGA West, has its headquarters in Los Angeles. Membership is on a national basis. The Writers Guild has sister guilds in the English-speaking countries—Great Britain, Canada, Australia, New Zealand. The exchange of information among the five guilds is of value to writers throughout the English-speaking world since co-productions, satellites, cables, and other forms of production cross international boundaries.

Applicants for membership must have at least two professional writing credits in the area of television, screen, or radio writing.

Manuscript Registration Service

The Guild's registration service has been set up to assist members and nonmembers of the Guild in establishing the completion date and the identity of their literary property. An author has certain rights under the law the moment his or her work is completed. It is important that the date of completion be legally established. Writers Guild of America, East, accepts for registration manuscripts as well as material not in full script form, that is, synopses, outlines, ideas, treatments, scenarios. A registration is valid for ten years and may be renewed.

Publications

Although there is not a regular publication, the Guild publishes a screen-format publication as an aid to screenwriters, as well as a membership directory.

Fee

The initiation fee is $500, and there are annual dues of $50, which may be paid $12.50 per quarter.

Foundation grants are given once a year for screen-writers. For further information contact the main office.

3. WOMEN'S AND MINORITY ORGANIZATIONS

American Indian Community House Gallery

Basement Workshop, Inc.

Center for Inter-American Relations

El Grupo Morivivi, Inc.

The Frank Silvera Writers' Workshop

Frederick Douglass Creative Arts Center, Inc.

Greek Cultural Center

Harlem Writers Guild

The Heresies Collective

International Women's Writing Guild

Midmarch Associates

New York Feminist Art Institute

Ollantay Center for the Arts

"Where We At" Black Women Artists, Inc.

Women's Interart Center

The Women's Salon

In this section are profiles of organizations representing and offering support to groups with special needs: Asian Americans, blacks, Greeks, Hispanics, American Indians, and women. Some groups are exclusive and some encourage multi-ethnic participation. Almost all organizations provide programs and services for all artists, including writers.

Note: This list represents an eclectic group of organizations. Omission of any group was not intentional.

AMERICAN INDIAN COMMUNITY HOUSE GALLERY
386 West Broadway, Second Floor
New York, NY 10012
(212) 226-7433

The American Indian Community House Gallery is a center for American Indian artists, musicians, and writers. The Gallery mounts five to six exhibitions annually of contemporary Native American or Eskimo art. Ongoing programs also include a poetry series, theater performances, musical programs, and a summer workshop space.

The American Indian Community House Lecture Program focuses on such topics as North American Indian Architecture and Art, Women in American Indian History, and Current Issues in American Indian Life. Call for information on current programs.

The Gallery offers career information and referrals.

"Keep working; when opportunity knocks talk is meaningless unless there's work to back up what you say."
—Advice from the Gallery

Although the Gallery membership is for Native Americans, anyone interested in Native American Indian culture is invited to the programs.

Publication

Native American Directory. A reference for locating organizations, events, and tribal offices and reserves. $16.95, plus $3. for shipping.

BASEMENT WORKSHOP, INC.
22 Catherine Street
New York, NY 10038
(212) 732-0770

Basement Workshop is a nonprofit Asian-American arts organization based in New York's Chinatown. The Workshop develops, produces, and promotes the works of Asian-Americans in the visual, performing, and literary arts.

Literature Program

Resident and guest writers lead workshops in poetry, prose, and play writing. In the fall 1982 season, workshops were given in performance poetry by Jessica Hagedorn and Lairie Carlos. In the same season, readings were given by Olga Broumas, Thulani Davis, and Carol Berge, among others.

Special projects include anthologies, oral histories, and the archival documentation of works created and performed at the Workshop.

Access is an ongoing panel and lecture program that concentrates on the experiences and accomplishments of Asian-American artists. Panels are made up of leaders in arts-services organizations and artists of the Asian-American community.

Scholarship Program

In addition to employing interns to assist in its daily activities, the Workshop actively solicits other arts organizations in the city for scholarships, and internships where young and emerging artists can attain training and work experience.

Fees

Workshops, $8 a session; readings, a voluntary contribution of $2.

CENTER FOR INTER-AMERICAN RELATIONS
680 Park Avenue
New York, NY 10021
(212) 249-8950

The Center for Inter-American Relations is a private, nonprofit organization whose purpose is to develop closer ties between cultures and societies of the Western Hemisphere. The programs it sponsors range from discussions of political and economic issues to cultural activities in art, music, literature, drama, and other disciplines. Local audiences for these events include representatives from business and finance, government, journalism, and academia, as well as the general public.

Its combined theater and gallery, Intar, located on Theater Row at 42nd Street is geared to presenting current Latin American art and drama.

Publications

In the literary field, the Center's activities include sponsoring the translation of Latin American works into English, arranging for writers to visit the Center and give readings and lectures, and publishing the *Review*, a journal focusing on literature and the arts.

Consult the Center for details.

Fees

Membership is $15 for students and $35 for the general public. Members receive the *Review*, a monthly calendar and agenda, invitations to all exhibits, and special discounts on catalogs and concert series.

EL GRUPO MORIVIVI, INC.
A Collective Cultural Experience
1671 Lexington Avenue
New York, NY 10029
(212) 289-9332
678-1128 (messages)

Contact for Poetry Project:
Sandra Maria Esteres,
(212) 733-2150

El Grupo Morivivi is a collective of multiethnic, largely bilingual visual and interdisciplinary artists, poets, musicians, dancers, and artisans, operating out of a storefront gallery/performance space in El Barrio. The Morivivi program draws upon the diversity of its members in presenting exhibits and cultural events of professional quality that are representative of lesser-known artistic traditions as well as emerging and avant-garde art forms. It serves the geographical community of El Barrio, which has a majority of Puerto Rican/Hispanic residents (although other ethnic groups are significantly represented— black Americans and West Indians, Italian Americans, and Koreans).

Readings

El Grupo Morivivi, Inc., presents regular poetry readings in Spanish and English that feature invited poets. Open readings usually follow. It has been able to pay small fees to readers this past year. Featured poets have included Piri Thomas, Sandra Maria Esteres, Charlie Chan, Fay Chiang, K. Curtis Lyle, Luis Mendez, Janine Pommy Vega, and Victor Hernandez Cruz. If you are interested in giving a reading, please send a biography, a sample of work, and follow up with a phone call. Writers are encouraged to submit proposals for future workshops and classes in gallery space and other sites.

For a small fee, space may be rented from El Grupo Morivivi to be used for rehearsals and performances and or seminars for conferences. Call to find out the particulars.

THE FRANK SILVERA WRITERS' WORKSHOP
317 West 125th Street, Third Floor
New York, NY 10027
(212) 662-8463

The primary purpose of the Frank Silvera Writers' Workshop is to offer support and guidance to new and relatively unknown playwrights—especially black playwrights—and to assist them in the development of their play writing skills. The focus of the Workshop is on the development of the playwright's craft, not on the quality of a particular play. Therefore, the writer's participation in the workshops is mandatory.

The Workshop's Reading and Critique Series began in October 1973, in memory of Frank Silvera, who made a literary impact in his own time. Since the Workshop's founding, the organization has developed a writers' laboratory, which presents over sixty new playwrights' works each year.

Members must be either playwrights, directors, actors, or theater technicians. Although there is no fee for membership, a fee is charged for the individual writing seminars led by prominent playwrights.

Workshops and Reading and Critique Sessions

These sessions are designed to give the playwright an opportunity to hear his or her play read by the Workshop's professional pool of actors. The reading series is held on Monday evenings at 7:30 and Saturday afternoons at 3:00. As mentioned before, the writers' participation is mandatory.

In order to qualify to participate in these readings, the writer must copyright and bind two completed copies of the play for the administrative staff. All readings are planned and rehearsed before the sessions.

The second stage of a new play's refinement takes place in a "rewrite reading session." Once a play is read during the initial critique, writers may schedule another reading of a play once it has been revised.

Playscripts are chosen by member directors for staged productions. Four plays from the Workshop are selected by these directors each season. The season runs from October to June.

Playwrights' Archive

The Library of the Living Playwright is a library that contains members' manuscripts and tapes of their readings and performances. The library's function is to bring alumni's plays to the attention of producers and directors. Viewing, copying, or borrowing a manuscript is not permitted without the writer's permission.

Publications

A monthly schedule of events is mailed to all people whose names are on the Workshop's mailing list.

Fees

There is no fee for membership. There are fees for the individual writing seminars. Consult the Workshop for details.

FREDERICK DOUGLASS CREATIVE ARTS CENTER, INC.
276 West 43rd Street
New York, N.Y. 10036
(212) 944-9870

The Frederick Douglass Creative Arts Center, Inc., is a nonprofit cultural and educational institution committed to the development of literary and performing artists and to the production and publication of high-quality artistic works. The Center's focus is as much on seeing its students strive for rich and rewarding careers as it is on refining their creative processes.

The activities of the Center are directed toward fostering the talent of black and third world artists, both performers and writers. The FDCAC sponsors a number of intermediate- and professional-level workshops in fiction, prose, poetry, drama, journalism, and film and TV writing, in addition to workshops in acting. The Center presents three plays a year, videotape programs, and The Black Roots Festival, an annual celebration of poetry and music. The noted author of *Tar Baby*, Toni Morrison, commented, "The future of black writing in America may very well depend on environments like the Frederick Douglass Creative Arts Center."

Workshops are open to anyone with the interest and the willingness to do creative work. Workshop sessions in the various genres are held on weekday evenings and on Saturdays.

Publications

The American Rag. A cultural journal of poetry, fiction, and the visual arts.

FDCAC Newsletter. Published semi annually; contains news on FDCAC events and lists workshop schedules.

GREEK CULTURAL CENTER
27-18 Hoyt Avenue South
Long Island City, NY 11102   **Contact: Adam Tourtoulis**
(212) 726-7329   **Ms. Eleni F. Paidoussi**

The Greek Cultural Center, located in Astoria, the heart of New York City's Greek community, has been in existence since 1974 and is sponsored by the New York State Council on the Arts and the Queens Council on the Arts. The Center is run under the auspices of the Greek Ministry of Culture. Through its various programs it offers the Greek community the opportunity to learn, to create, and to retain roots, language, and identity.

The Center specializes in theater, literature, ethnic dances and music, shadow theater, and film festivals. Their productions range from major presentations with thousands in the audience to small-scaled informal productions, seminars, and workshops.

The services provided to Greek writers include counseling, referral, and advice on technical and publishing possibilities. Writers are also given opportunities to read poetry, literature, and plays. Apprentices help with publication and arts administration.

Publications

Stohoi ("Aims") is a quarterly literature/information/folk arts magazine.

> "Write *what* you feel the *way* you feel *when* you feel."
> —advice from the Center

HARLEM WRITERS GUILD
372 Central Park West, Suite 19J
New York, NY 10025
(212) 866-0095

During the last thirty-five years, the Harlem Writers Guild has offered services to writers that include seminars, book parties, and opportunities for publication. Presently the Guild is organizing an anthology that will include the works of Guild alumni and current members. The organization is designed to serve the black and Hispanic writers of the Harlem community.

Guild members participate in workshops and readings for the purpose of helpful and mutual criticism.

Unlike other literary guilds, the Harlem Writers Guild does not co-sign and secure contracts for its membership.

Eligibility

Writers should have demonstrable skills in either fiction or drama. Samples of work should be submitted to the Guild for consideration.

Fees

The minimum annual membership dues are $30. There is a sliding scale for students and nonworking members.

THE HERESIES COLLECTIVE, INC.
P.O. Box 766, Canal Street Station
New York, NY 10013
(212) 431-9060

The Heresies Collective, Inc., is a nonprofit cultural organization that publishes the journal *Heresies: A Feminist Publication on Art and Politics*, holds technical workshops, and organizes talks and performances. The Heresies Collective is composed of women artists, writers, and political activists.

Each issue of *Heresies* focuses on a specific theme. Recent issues were devoted to women's sexuality, the environment, women's organizing, architecture and living space, music, and the development of new art forms such as page art. The Collective actively recruits women artists for the editorial collective, which solicits, edits, and designs each issue under the Collective's auspices. The magazine has from the beginning sought to merge the work and writing of women artists with those of poets, polemicists, journalists, and critics.

The Collective also provides internships for women students interested in feminist networking, publishing, and art. Inquiries from prospective interns are welcomed.

The Heresies Collective provides women artists with an environment where their ideas and their work are taken seriously on both aesthetic and political levels. Their Collective statement professes this philosophy: "Our view of feminism is one of process and change, and we feel that in the process of this dialogue we can foster a change in the meaning of art."

Back issues of *Heresies* can be obtained for $6 each. Forthcoming issues will focus on the media, women's organizations, women in theater, and mother/daughter relationships and class. The newsstand price is $5 per copy. Subscriptions are $15 for one year and $27 for two years for individuals, and $24 for one year and $44 for two years for institutions.

INTERNATIONAL WOMEN'S WRITING GUILD
P.O. Box 810, Gracie Station
New York, NY 10028
(212) 737-7536

Founded in 1976, the International Women's Writing Guild is an alliance open to all aspiring or accomplished women writers interested in expressing themselves through the written word professionally and for personal growth. The IWWG sponsors an annual week-long writing conference at Skidmore College in Saratoga Springs, New York, that is attended by about three hundred women from every part of the U.S., Canada, and abroad. More than thirty workshops are offered at this conference.

Eligibility

Membership is open to "any woman connected to the written word, regardless of professional portfolio." Members write fiction, poetry, drama, and articles for magazines, newspapers, and journals.
The Guild facilitates manuscript submissions to New York literary agents; conducts a talent bank, a job-placement effort to place women in writing-related work; has access to the archival repository at the Sophia Smith Collection on the History of Women at Smith College for the deposit of seminal materials written by individual members. Most importantly, the Guild offers a supportive network to all struggling women writers.

Publications

Network. Member newsletter, published six times a year.
Monographs: "Writing as an Act of Faith"
"The Ethics of Writing: Conflict With Conscience"
"Hope, Courage, Inspiration and Creativity"

Fees

Annual membership dues: $20
Foreign memberships: $26

> "Stay in good health, for you will probably have to do two or more full-time things: to make a living and to write."
> —Advice from the Guild

MIDMARCH ASSOCIATES
P.O. Box 3304
Grand Central Station
New York, NY 10017
(212) 666-6990

Midmarch Associates is a women's arts-service organization that plans and coordinates exhibitions, conferences, festivals, and symposia, as well as publishes books on the arts and *Women Artists News*. It maintains internship programs and an information clearinghouse and resource center that contains information on grants, schools, and technical consultation.

Publications

Women Artists News is a bimonthly publication about women and the arts and an excellent source of information on the subject; it includes reviews of exhibitions, shows, books, films, reports on conferences, interviews, and feature articles. It is the official information conduit for the International Organization of Women in the Arts.

Two books are also published by Midmarch: *Guide to Women's Arts Organizations* and *Voices of Women: Three Critics on Three Poets*.

Write to the above address for more information on subscription fees and ordering books.

NEW YORK FEMINIST ART INSTITUTE
325 Spring Street
New York, NY 10013
(212) 242-1343

A feminist art school, devoted largely to the visual arts and art history, the New York Feminist Art Institute offers some writing classes in its curriculum. The purpose of the school is to foster and develop a truly feminist aesthetic by giving women "a room of their own" where they can focus on art and pursue other women's studies. Included are drawing, painting, photography, sculpture, women's art history, analytical thinking, consciousness raising, performance art, and journal writing.

The Institute's Hatch-Billops Collection documents visual, performing, and literary arts, concentrating on contemporary and traditional black artists.

Internships/Apprenticeships

Internships are available to work with women artist professionals in the New York community and in arranging the women's art-slide registry from Lucy Lippard's Collection.

Fees

Any woman interested can take workshops of courses. The minimum fee is $20. The application for the Institute contains all the relevant information.

OLLANTAY CENTER FOR THE ARTS
P.O. Box 4105
Sunnyside, NY 11104
or
87-03 Northern Boulevard
Jackson Heights, NY 11372
(212) 565-6499

Ollantay Center for the Arts is a community-based arts organization that sponsors various cultural programs for the Hispanic community of Jackson Heights.

In the literary field, the Center sponsors lectures, workshops, and panel discussions with writers in Spanish. With the Literary Arts Division of the Queens Council on the Arts, the Center publishes *Source*, which is bilingual and serves as a forum for writers of poetry and prose in Spanish who reside in the New York area.

In addition to several readings every season, Ollantay sponsors lectures by professors and well-known writers, panel discussions with published writers and poets, and a playwright's workshop. Consult Ollantay for schedule and details.

Publications

Source. Published annually, with Queens Councils on the Arts. (See separate listing.)

Fees

Regular annual membership dues, $10; sustaining, $120.

"One of the latest waves of immigrants to come to the United States is that of Hispanics from the various countries of Latin America. Ollantay Center for the Arts has discovered that this group houses excellent writers and poets who write in Spanish and whose work cannot gain exposure because of the language barrier. The Literary Program of Ollantay is geared to provide encouragement and assistance to meet some of the needs of these writers."
—Statement from Ollantay

"WHERE WE AT" BLACK WOMEN ARTISTS, INC.
154 Crown Street
Brooklyn, NY 11225
(212) 756-1897

"Where We At" is a group of black female artists dedicated not only to the enrichment of its members but to bringing cultural and creative awareness to the whole community. Founded in 1971, the organization has exhibited locally, nationally, and internationally. Members include painters, printmakers, photographers, writers, craftspersons, sculptors, illustrators, muralists, performers, and gallery owners.

Art workshops, seminars, and slide lectures on black art are conducted regularly.

A brochure on the history and direction of the organization is available upon request. Call or write for more information.

WOMEN'S INTERART CENTER
549 West 52nd Street
New York, NY 10019
(212) 246-1050

The Women's Interart Center is a nonprofit multiarts institution that promotes the work of women artists in many disciplines. It provides facilities and services in theater, film, video, visual arts, dance, and music under one roof to encourage collaboration and cross-fertilization. Membership and professional training in theater, film, and video are open to men and women.

Theater Program

A member of the New York Alliance for Resident Theaters (formerly the Off-Off Broadway Alliance), the Interart Theatre produces three to six full-scale productions each season involving women playwrights, directors, and designers whose talents have in many cases been overlooked by male theater producers. Subsequent reviews and professional notice of their work enabled many of these women to launch promising careers in the commercial and nonprofit theater communities.

The Center also sponsors the New York performances of the Women's Experimental Theatre, a seven-year-old company that collaboratively develops and performs works on subjects of interest to women.

The Center offers many professional training courses in writing for film, stage, and video, plus special conferences and colloquia on interdisciplinary collaboration. Playwrights-in-residence assist novice playwrights.

College-accredited, integrated media programs (one full-year) plus special courses in writing, directing, and TV production for film and video are taught at the Center.

Internships are available. Contact Jere Jacobs for more information.

Fees

Membership is open to all men and women, and dues are $35 yearly. It includes mailings of upcoming events, free admissions, and 20 percent discounts on other presentations. To be put on their mailing list, contact the Director of Development, Jere Jacobs.

> "A writer for performance arts functions most effectively in a collaborative environment where he/she can participate fully in a work-in-progress and can call on the specialized talents of others to enhance the work."
> —Statement from the Center

THE WOMEN'S SALON
436 West Street, Apt. 933B
New York, NY 10014
(212) 691-0539   Contact: Erika Duncan

The Women's Salon is an alternative literary network that provides audience support and serious critical attention to new works by women. In addition to holding monthly public readings and two open readings a year, the Salon conducts two fiction and autobiographical workshops that meet once a week, on Sunday mornings and Wednesday evenings.

The readings and programs offer opportunities for writers to hear speakers and readers from other parts of the world and to be exposed to ideas not generally aired. The Sunday and Wednesday workshops provide a small supportive atmosphere in which to explore simultaneous growth in the craft of writing and the use of personal exploration in the process.

The Salon's program of readings includes new works and talks by women of interest to the whole community. Recently Tillie Olsen spoke to workshop participants about Ding Ling, a Chinese woman writer. In November 1982, Norma Alarcon, the editor of *Third Woman,* organized a meeting on the literary and graphic work of Hispanic women living and writing on the East Coast at which Sandra Esteves, Luz Maria Umpierre, and Marjorie Agosin read from their own works.

This is a statewide organization, but mailings are national and international.

Fees

There is a yearly membership fee of $15. Members may attend all programs free of charge and receive bimonthly mailings of the Salon's newsletter.

Student internships are available in helping with all aspects of the Salon's activities. Call for further information.

4. COMMUNITY COUNCILS

Bronx Council on the Arts

Brooklyn Arts and Culture Association

Harlem Cultural Council

Lower Manhattan Cultural Council

Queens Council on the Arts

Staten Island Council on the Arts

The councils mentioned in this section provide valuable services and programs in their communities, including newsletters and calendars with information of borough, citywide, and even national interest; and counseling on grants, careers, and arts programs. Some councils also offer the writer the possibility of conducting workshops and readings.

BRONX COUNCIL ON THE ARTS
2114 Williamsbridge Road
Bronx, NY 10461
(212) 931-9500

The Bronx Council on the Arts (BCA) is a community-based arts-service organization that provides to its constituency in the Bronx arts-related services in a variety of disciplines, including workshops and services for writers.

The BCA Writers Workshop is a program of weekly sessions held at the BCA offices and other Bronx locations. Fiction, poetry, nonfiction, tips on getting work published, and information on contemporary trends in the field are some of the topics covered. In addition to the Writers Workshop, there are mini-workshops in specialized areas of writing taught by guest writers, and these culminate in readings by participants. Examples of these events are creative-writing workshops for senior citizens and high school students, lectures on play-writing technique, and seminars on publishing.

A critic-at-large service has been established for those who cannot attend any of the workshops at their scheduled times. Writer-in-residence Yvonne, a poet, an editor, and a teacher at Hunter College and New York University, will review up to twenty pages of a writer's prose or poetry and will return material with her critiques. Writers may send material, along with a self-addressed stamped envelope, to the above address.

The BCA also has a resource packet available that includes information on workshops, publishing, grants, and how to submit materials for publication.

Publications

Bronx Arts is a monthly newsletter that provides a listing of events in the Bronx that are not covered by the metropolitan dailies. The newsletter also describes arts services and resources available to arts groups and individuals. To receive the newsletter, write to the above address and ask to be put on the mailing list.

BROOKLYN ARTS AND CULTURE ASSOCIATION
200 Eastern Parkway
Brooklyn, NY 11238
(212) 783-3077

The Brooklyn Arts and Culture Association (BACA) is composed of a membership of more than 35,000 civic, community, educational, cultural, and business institutions as well as individuals devoted to promoting cultural programs within the borough.

BACA is designated by the New York State Council on the Arts and the New York City Department of Cultural Affairs as the agency to handle its regranting funds, up to $3,000 a grant, for Brooklyn's community arts organizations.

The Brooklyn Arts and Culture Association

- assists in the establishment of new community cultural centers and groups and aids existing cultural community programs.

- promotes development and training of the gifted child and adult in professional art field.

- provides art exhibitions and entertainment throughout Brooklyn.

- serves as a liaison between the borough's cultural and educational institutions and their community-oriented programs.

- promotes summer festival and cultural events in Brooklyn's parks and communities.

- serves as a clearinghouse of the community's cultural needs by supplying groups with information, services, workshops, lectures, bookkeeping, publicity, and needed exposure.

- publishes a monthly calendar of cultural events throughout Brooklyn, mailed to BACA's membership.

The Council sponsors writing and drama workshops for children and teenagers at the Downtown Center, where work is both written and performed. The BACA also sponsors poetry and theater readings at the Brooklyn Museum every Sunday from October through June. Some programs feature readings by well-known guest authors and poets, and others are readings open to the general public.

Publications

A monthly calendar of cultural events in Brooklyn is published containing valuable information about Brooklyn-based organizations and programs of interest to writers. For example, from their October 1982 calendar:

MENWEM WRITERS WORKSHOP. A continuing series of workshops, readings, and development of cultural resources. For information: Ms. Brenda Connor-Bey, 136 Cambridge Place, Brooklyn, NY 11238.

NEW PAUL ROBESON CULTURAL CENTER. Programs in all artistic disciplines. The Cultural Center is predominantly concerned with the black aesthetic and experience and provides space for classes, rehearsals, readings, performances, and other events. For more information, call 622-6227 (Tuesday, 6–9) or 282-8327 (Thursday).

BOOK GATHERINGS, INC. Encouragement of book as an art form. Festivals and multimedia events are held. For more information, contact Susan Share at (212) 852-3875.

CREATIVE WRITING GROUP. For senior citizens interested in writing original poems, essays, and playlets. For information, contact the East Flatbush YM–YWHA Senior Center, 648 Remsen Avenue at Avenue A, 345-0222.

THE UNIVERSAL BLACK WRITER. An information-sharing publication that seeks work by black writers of poetry for reading by and for blacks, publishers interested in materials by and for blacks, and other relevant news. All inquiries should be directed to Linda Cousins, Editor, Universal Black Writer, P.O. Box 5, Radio City Station, New York, NY 10101.

Fees

Membership in BACA is $5.00 a year for individuals and $25 for organizations. Members receive the monthly calendar and newsletter. Call for further information.

HARLEM CULTURAL COUNCIL
1 West 125th Street, Room 206
New York, NY 10027
(212) 860-8640

Founded in 1964 as a community arts council, the Harlem Cultural Council provides services to professional minority artists, the general public, and creative arts programs. It sponsors major art exhibitions of historical and contemporary focus and educational programs for Harlem schools. Programs encompass performances as well as exhibitions of the plastic arts. The Council presents Dancemobile and a regular series of films.

The Council also serves as an information and referral service for artists and organizations of most disciplines in the areas of grants for arts activities.

The monthly newsletter, *Harlem Cultural Review,* reviews plans and dance concerts and publishes information helpful to minority artists.

Fees

Membership varies from $5 to $20 depending on the kind of membership. Members receive the newsletter and are entitled to reduced prices to events.

LOWER MANHATTAN CULTURAL COUNCIL
32 Broadway
New York, NY 10004
(212) 269-0320

The Lower Manhattan Cultural Council (LMCC) is an independent and nonprofit organization designed to coordinate and sponsor cultural events in Lower Manhattan.

LMCC supports and promotes performances, readings, and exhibitions. Past events that the Council sponsored include sculpture and video installations, outdoor music and theater, and readings.

The Council's Arts Advisory Services provides advice to arts organizations and individual artists on matters of administration, technical assistance, development, promotion, publicity, permits, and performance locations and space.

Publications

Downtown, the monthly newsletter of the LMCC, publishes information on the cultural activities in Lower Manhattan, including a calendar of events in all disciplines. The subscription rate is $5 a year.

The Council also publishes a guide to downtown performance and exhibition spaces. Consult above address for details.

QUEENS COUNCIL ON THE ARTS
161-04 Jamaica Avenue
Jamaica, NY 11432
(212) 291-1100

The Queens Council on the Arts (QCA) is a community-based arts-service organization that serves the artistic community and general population of Queens by sponsoring public arts programs and offering financial support, technical assistance, and publicity.

The QCA Literary Arts Division provides opportunities for poets and writers to give readings—especially bilingual readings—and conduct workshops throughout the borough of Queens. It produces chapbooks and a small-press magazine called *Source*. With York College, the Literary Arts Division sponsors an annual high school literary contest and participates in the PEN project.

Nonprofit cultural groups of every discipline in Queens may apply to the Cosponsorship Support Program for financial help. Even programs devised by individual artists may receive grants from the QCA as long as a not-for-profit organization applies on their behalf. Application guidelines and forms and information on deadlines are available from the QCA office.

The Literary Arts Division's programs include twelve readings throughout Queens each year, printing and graphic design services for small publications, and the annual publication of *Source,* the QCA's official literary magazine.

The QCA cosponsors conferences, workshops, and seminars with other local and citywide cultural groups. These are largely concerned with administrative subjects and fund-raising strategies pertaining to cultural groups, and so they encompass artistic disciplines other than the literary arts.

Publications

Source, published in cooperation with Ollantay Center for the Arts, features poetry and fiction by nationally known as well as promising Queens writers. Published in Spanish and English, it often contains the work of contemporary Latin American writers currently residing in Queens. *Source* welcomes poetry, essays, fiction, reviews, graphics, and photography. A single issue is $2, plus fifty cents for postage.

QCA "Your Information" Newsletter is published monthly and focuses on grants and career information. It contains announcements of new programs of arts-services organizations, new publications useful to arts organizations and individual artists and writers, developments in national and statewide funding procedures, and more. A regular feature is the QCA Jobline, which lists positions in the arts and arts administration. This newsletter is available to QCA's members.

Queens Leisure Guide is published seasonally and lists all of the artistic happenings in Queens. The guide is sent to members.

Fees

Membership dues are $3 for students and senior citizens, $5 for individuals, $15 for family, $25 for sponsors, $50 for patrons, and $100 for sustaining.

> "Cuts in government spending have severely hurt programs supporting literary arts. We must join together not only to protest the cutbacks but to demand quality programs. To continue the present course of events will result in a nation of illiterates."
> —Statement from the QCA

(See also Ollantay Center for the Arts—another local Queens organization.)

STATEN ISLAND COUNCIL ON THE ARTS
c/o Pouch Terminal
1 Edgewater Street
Staten Island, NY 10305
(212) 448-7877

The Staten Island Council on the Arts provides financial support and technical assistance to small arts groups of all disciplines and acts as an information clearinghouse. At present, the Council is developing programs for writers.

Publications

For Art's Sake, the monthly arts newspaper published by the Council, features listings of cultural events in Staten Island as well as in New York City and throughout the state. This newsletter is distributed free in Staten Island.

For more information about membership services, write to the Council at the above address.

Fees

Membership dues are $10, $25, and $50 for individuals and $100 for organizations.

5. INFORMATION CLEARINGHOUSES

Association of Hispanic Arts, Inc.

Center for Arts Information

The Foundation Center

Foundation for the Community of Artists

Rewrite

The organizations in this chapter are important resource centers for writers and other artists. The Foundation Center has a library of grants information for organizations and individual artists. The Center for Arts Information and the Association of Hispanic Arts have comprehensive libraries with information available on fellowships, grants services, surveys, and the arts to organizations, artists, and students. The Foundation for the Community of Artists offers information on many subjects by phone.

All these organizations publish informative brochures and periodicals, which may be ordered directly from them.

ASSOCIATION OF HISPANIC ARTS, INC.
200 East 87th Street, 2nd Floor
New York, NY 10028
(212) 369-7054

The Association of Hispanic Arts (AHA), although not exclusively a literary service organization, disseminates and gathers enough information on all of the Hispanic arts to make it a worthwhile resource for those interested in Hispanic literary activities. The AHA's facilities and publications provide an abundance of information on events, small arts organizations, grants, and current funding practices pertinent to the Hispanic artistic worker. The AHA conducts workshops and conferences on funding resources and offers instruction on acquiring fund-raising skills.

The AHA's bimonthly newsletter, *Hispanic Arts,* has a directory of Hispanic arts groups and service organizations. Although this newsletter usually contains more information on the performing and visual arts, it does not exclude the literary arts. There are articles about writers, and each issue contains announcements about which theater companies are soliciting plays written in Spanish.

The AHA's Central Information Office is open daily to the general public and provides information services on funding and job opportunities.

The Funding Resource Library is open to organizations, artists, and students and has information on fellowships, grants, public relations, community services, surveys, and arts-related material.

Referral services on legal and administrative matters are provided on request, and individual technical assistance is provided by appointment.

Publications

Hispanic Arts Newsletter, published bimonthly, covers funding issues and regularly prints announcements on manuscript solicitations and grant deadlines and a directory of Hispanic arts organizations.

AHA Funding Directory, published by the AHA's Funding Research and Development Project, lists foundations, corporations, and public arts-funding opportunities for individual artists and arts organizations.

Cartelera Mensual is a monthly calendar of events published in Spanish.

Fees

The AHA is asking for donations toward the publication of *Hispanic Arts Newsletter*. Suggested donations are $6 from individuals and $10 from organizations for five issues annually. Your contribution is tax-deductible.

CENTER FOR ARTS INFORMATION
625 Broadway
New York, NY 10012
(212) 677-7548

The Center for Arts Information is a major clearinghouse for information useful to nonprofit organizations and artists in all disciplines, including writers. It maintains a 5,500-volume reference library, receives 325 arts-related periodicals, and produces a number of publications of use to writers.

Visits to the library require an appointment made by phone at least one day prior to the visit. The library contains files on nonprofit service organizations and literary societies and groups throughout the city and nation and a wealth of information on subjects such as cultural exchanges, colonies, grants, careers, and copyright information.

Publications

A complete list of publications is available from the Center. The following publications focus on subjects relevant to writers.

Artist Colonies. Information on 24 artist retreats located in the United States, classified by discipline. 1982, $1.50.

Careers in the Arts: A Resource Guide. A guide to professional unions, associations, internships, apprenticeships, and training programs to help individuals make the necessary and proper choices about arts careers. Co-published with Opportunity Resources for the Arts. 1981, $6.75.

International Cultural Exchange. A guide to 57 organizations that facilitate or fund international cultural exchange programs. Includes brief bibliography. 1981, $2.50.

Jobs in the Arts and Arts Administration. A guide to placement and referral services, career counseling, and publications that feature arts-employment listings. 1981, $2.

Money for Artists. A guide to grants, awards, fellowships, and artists-in-residence programs primarily for the New York State artist; bibliographic references useful nationally. 1980, $2.

A Quick Guide to Loans and Emergency Funds. Describes six free or arts-loan funds for organizations in New York and two special bank programs, as well as 14 loan or emergency funds for artists. 1982, $2.

Copyright. A pamphlet for writers and artists on the subject. Free.

Nonprofit Status in New York State. A guide explaining nonprofit status relating to groups and individuals. Free.

To receive free publications, please send a self-addressed stamped envelope.

THE FOUNDATION CENTER
888 Seventh Avenue
New York, NY 10106
(800) 434-9836 (for full-order information on publications)
(212) 975-1120 (for Manhattan library)

The Foundation Center is a nationwide service organization that collects and publishes information on private foundations and other philanthropic organizations throughout the United States. Its central office and library are in midtown Manhattan, and it has two field offices in Cleveland and San Francisco. It maintains subsidiary collections in local libraries across the United States and a national collection in Washington, DC. The addresses of the other national centers are given below.

Details on private foundations that the Center offers include deadlines and guidelines for grants applications, history of grants recipients, tax records, and the members of boards. Although the Center's main body of material is useful only to nonprofit organizations, its publication, *Foundation Grants to Individuals,* is of particular interest to individual writers.

The Library in New York

The Center's Manhattan branch maintains a collection of publications that list the whereabouts of writers' colonies, exchange programs, prizes, and marketing information. Many of the books listed in the bibliography of this book are in the library's collection.

Publications

Foundation Grants to Individuals. Describes programs of more than 900 foundations that make grants to individuals. $15.

Indexes to Foundation Grants

Foundation Grants Index, annual volume. Subject index to more than 19,000 foundation grants per year. $27.

COMSEARCH Printouts: Subjects. Computer printouts listing grants in specific categories of giving. $12 per subject (microfiche ed., $4).

COMSEARCH Printouts: Geographic. Computer printouts listing grants to recipients in specific states and cities. $25 for New York City and for California; $15 all others (microfiche eds., $8/$5).

COMSEARCH Printouts: Special topics. Computer printouts listing foundations by asset and grant size and grouping community and operating foundations. $12 per printout (microfiche ed., $4).

Guides for Grant Seekers

Foundation Fundamentals, Fall 1980. Guide to foundations and funding research. $4.95.

Philanthropy in the United States: History and Structure. $1.50.

What Will a Foundation Look for When You Submit a Grant Proposal? Up to five copies free.

What Makes a Good Proposal? Up to five copies may be obtained free.

Special Topics

Directory of Evaluation Consultants, Fall 1980. Information on more than 550 experts in program evaluation. $8.95.

Conducting Evaluations: Three Perspectives. Fall 1980, Three papers plus bibliography on the evaluation process. $2.95.

Other Foundation Center Libraries

The other national collection is in Washington, DC. The address is 1001 Connecticut Avenue, N.W., Suite 938, Washington, DC, 20036; telephone (202) 331-1400.

The addresses of the two field offices in San Francisco and Cleveland are:

312 Sutter Street
San Francisco, CA 94108
(415) 397-0902

739 National City Bank Building
629 Euclid Avenue
Cleveland, OH 44114
(216) 861-1933

For a complete address list of regional collections, call (800) 424-9836.

FOUNDATION FOR THE COMMUNITY OF ARTISTS
280 Broadway, Suite 412
New York, NY 10007
(212) 227-3770   **Contact: Tim Smith**

The Foundation for the Community of Artists is a nonprofit membership service directed to improving the social and economic situation of artists.

The FCA assists artists in dealing with many issues, including unemployment, occupational safety, housing, artists' rights, law, business, and arts legislation.

The services that address these issues are:

Artists' Hotline. An information and referral service that counsels artists on legal matters, employment, and careers. The number of this hotline is (212) 285-2121.

Artists' Housing Hotline. Specifically for questions on artists' housing. The telephone number is (212) 285-2133. The hotline gives assistance with tenant organizing and counseling; information on city and private agencies; and legal referrals. Housing listings are not available.

Blue Cross/Blue Shield Health Plan. Medical coverage to members of the FCA who are residents of the metropolitan area is available at a discount. More than 400 participants are enrolled in this health plan.

Foundation Graphics. A typesetting and graphic-design shop is available that provides design and type services to artists, nonprofit agencies, and commercial accounts.

Seminar Program. Five seminars have been conducted since 1978 in conjunction with the Small Business Administration and the National Endowment for the Arts. Topics of the seminars have included survival skills, business, and housing.

Publications

Art and Artists (formerly *Artworkers' News*) is a monthly newspaper that focuses on questions of survival, such as housing, law, occupational hazards, funding careers, and art education. It can be purchased at many newsstands for $1.25 per copy. The subscription rate is $12.50 per year.

Artists' Update is a calendar of events sponsored by Artists' Hotline. It is published monthly and is free with a self-addressed stamped envelope.

Fees

Membership is open to artists of any discipline. Individual membership is $17.50, which includes a subscription to FCA publications.

REWRITE
York College, Jamaica, NY 11451

(212) REW-RITE

This telephone number is a grammar hotline. Anyone can receive immediate information about writing problems by calling the above number from 1:00 P.M. to 4:00 P.M. every weekday. The hotline will be answered by a member of the English faculty of York College or of a New York City high school.

People interested in hearing sample problems can listen to the radio station WNYE, 91.5 FM, Tuesdays at 7:30 P.M. and Wednesdays at 10:00 A.M. when REWRITE reviews interesting requests.

PART II: SPECIAL OPPORTUNITIES FOR WRITERS

6. CAREER DEVELOPMENT AND JOB OPTIONS

Artists Career Planning Service

Associated Writing Programs

New York City Urban Corps

New York State Artists-in-Residence Program

New York State Council on the Arts' Internship/Apprenticeship
  Program

Opportunity Resources for the Arts

Poets in the Schools

The Script Development Workshop

Teachers and Writers Collaborative

The Writers Community, Inc.

The profiles in this section provide information to help you with
career decisions: information about apprenticeships, internships,
workshops, and alternative-job considerations. Some organizations
listed in the first part of this book also offer career advice and information, especially for women and minorities. Consult the individual profiles.

ARTISTS CAREER PLANNING SERVICE
434 Avenue of the Americas
New York, NY 10011
(212) 460-8163   **Contact: Peggie Lowenberg**

The Artists Career Planning Service (ACPS) was established in 1981 to provide career planning and assistance on matters of marketing and employment for the New York artistic community, with a particular (although not exclusive) commitment to recent graduates, women, and minorities.

ACPS professional counseling is open to artists of all disciplines. Clients receive assistance in the areas of grant applications, résumé writing, portfolios, marketing strategies, confidence building, resources and referrals, skills assessment, and setting of goals.

> "ACPS helps all artists who are ready to work on surviving and succeeding in the long run; it is a reality-based service which offers personalized counseling and group workshops at a reasonable fee."
> —Statement from the Service

Artists should call (212) 460-8163 to arrange an initial consultation and obtain information on current services and fees. The office is open by appointment only.

ASSOCIATED WRITING PROGRAMS
c/o Old Dominion University
Norfolk, VA 23508
(804) 440-3839

The Associated Writing Programs (AWP) was founded in 1967 in order to support creative-writing programs at colleges and universities throughout the country. Since that time it has become a major support organization for individual writers by assisting its members in their professional development, by helping members locate jobs, and by fostering a healthy environment for the survival of writers through publications, advocacy, and information.

Membership in the AWP is open to individual writers and creative-writing programs at colleges and universities across the country.

Writers are assisted in locating writer-in-residencies and full-time writer/teacher positions through listings as well as through the *AWP Newsletter.*

In each issue the AWP Newsletter prints manuscript requests from small presses and announcements of importance to creative-writing students and professionals regarding awards, contests, and so on. The newsletter, issued ten times during the year, reports on AWP conferences and publishes articles and announcements related to teaching, writing, and publishing.

Fees

Annual membership dues are $220 for institutions and $20 for individuals. The subscription rate for the *AWP Newsletter* is $7 a year.

NEW YORK CITY URBAN CORPS
32 Worth Street
New York, NY 10013
(212) 566-3952

The New York City Urban Corps is the nation's first and largest off-campus public-service internship program in municipal government for students in colleges, universities, and other higher-education institutions. It is sponsored cooperatively by the City of New York and the participating schools.

The guiding philosophy of the Urban Corps is to offer college students a work experience that will enhance their academic and career objectives. The Urban Corps program is a staffing resource for city agencies that can utilize motivated college students to assist in the delivery of city services.

In 1974 the New York City Department of Cultural Affairs initiated a broader placement of the Urban Corps Work/Study students within the cultural sector, with creative artists and arts organizations receiving city support. About 100 students a semester are placed in work-study assignment with arts organizations representing every discipline. To participate, schools must sign a yearly (June 1 to May 31) work-study agreement with the City of New York (Urban Corps). The city's share is derived from college aid budgeted lines converted for Urban Corps use. Colleges interested in participating in the program should write or call.

Students who desire to work in the New York City Urban Corps in a CWSP paid position, full- or part-time, must apply for the College Work Study Program at their school's financial aid office. If eligible for a CWSP grant, the student can request to work in the Urban Corps, provided that the school has signed a work-study agreement with the City of New York.

For arts organizations, eligibility to have paid work-study students is based on city support.

For further information, call Claire Tankel at (212) 974-1150.

NEW YORK STATE ARTISTS-IN-RESIDENCE PROGRAM
(formerly Artists-in-Schools)
New York Foundation for the Arts
5 Beekman Street
New York, NY 10038
(212) 233-3900

The New York State Artists-in-Residence Program (NYS-AIR) is part of the National Endowment for the Arts Artists-in-Education Program. Through the NYS-AIR Program, professional artists are placed in a number of educational, cultural, and community settings throughout New York City and New York State. The artists' residencies serve the purpose of acquainting the community with artistic activity.

Residencies are available in literature and the performing arts as well as in the visual arts. Depending on the artistic discipline, a residency can last from three weeks to a full school year.

The New York Foundation maintains a résumé file of professional artists of all disciplines who are interested in working in educational settings. Files are reviewed once a year by the Foundation's selection panel, which is comprised of artists and arts administrators.

Applicants who are selected by the Foundation panel are placed on an artists' roster, which is then distributed to the settings that wish to secure artists for residencies. An applicant is interviewed by a panel of community representatives and local professional artists from each setting.

Artists who wish to register for this program should contact the above address for an application form. Visual artists should include (with their applications) three to eight slides and a professional résumé. Contact the New York Foundation for the Arts at the above address for current deadlines.

The Foundation maintains information on employment options in educational settings such as schools, museums, arts organizations, and community centers. For further information, call (212) 233-3900.

The Foundation also conducts periodic seminars and workshops.

NEW YORK STATE COUNCIL ON THE ARTS' INTERNSHIP/APPRENTICESHIP PROGRAM
80 Centre Street
New York, NY 10013
(212) 587-4592

The New York State Council on the Arts is an important contributor of public funding for the arts. It receives an annual appropriation to be granted to the state's various nonprofit arts organizations applicants. It sets guidelines and criteria that have to be met for receiving funds.

The New York State Council on the Arts does not have a formal internship, apprenticeship, or volunteer program. Interested individuals and institutions, however, may develop a program tailored to their specific fields of interest. An intern working with the Council is taken behind the scenes and gains first-hand knowledge of the arts-funding process, a most valuable tool for those interested in pursuing a career in arts management and administration.

The Council has four divisions encompassing thirteen programs. They are *Administrative and Managerial* (administrative services, contract administration, public relations); *Programming and Fiscal Analysts* in the disciplines of communication arts (film, literature, media); *Performing Arts* (dance, musical presentation organizations, theater), including special programs in arts service organizations, special arts services, folk arts; and *Visual Arts* (architectural planning and design, museum aid, visual artists programs).

Internship programs usually can be tailored to accommodate the length of time and basic requirements for school credit where applicable.

Apprenticeships are more properly defined as renewable professional-service relations in which school credit is not granted.

Volunteer programs involve a professional commitment of specific days and hours extended on a ninety-day renewable basis.

All applicants are required to file applications and résumés to ensure effective placement. Questions may be clarified by telephone, but no candidate will be accepted without a selective interview with the Director of Staff Support Services and a department head.

Because of the Council's limited resources, stipends are not available for internships. Call for further details and application guidelines.

OPPORTUNITY RESOURCES FOR THE ARTS
1501 Broadway
New York, NY 10036
(212) 575-1688

Opportunity Resources for the Arts (OR) is a professional search firm that places individuals qualified in arts management or administration with cultural institutions and nonprofit arts organizations throughout the United States. OR also places writers in positions of editors, writers, researchers, and librarians, although most of its placements are in arts administration and arts business. Applicants must have at least two years of significant work experience in the types of jobs for which they apply. Pay scales range from ten to fifty thousand dollars. An applicant for OR registration must submit a detailed résumé and minimum salary requirements before the staff decides whether registration is appropriate. Registration does not guarantee placement.

If an applicant is accepted for placement registration, he or she must provide three references from previous employers and fill out a registration form describing employment history and geographical preferences.

Opportunity Resources also conducts a series of seminars on careers and publishes booklets on résumé writing and employment trends.

Publications

OR publishes pamphlets on résumé writing, employment trends, and listings of museums and arts-service organizations. Write OR for publications and price list.

Fees

Applicants pay an individual registration fee of $20.

POETS IN THE SCHOOLS
24 North Greeley Avenue
Chappaqua, NY 10514
(914) 238-4481
(212) 731-6611 (New York City office)

Poets in the Schools (PITS) is one of a number of organizations based in New York State that arrange for poets to teach in residencies in elementary and junior high schools. Residencies range from six and one-half to ten and one-half days, and the participating school provides at least $550 for each six-and-one-half-day period. Residencies are also supplemented by state and federal funds.

There are more poets who apply to PITS than there are available residencies, but PITS keeps a waiting list of those whose work has been screened by its reading panel.

When there is an opening and an applicant has been approved by the panel, he or she is then interviewed by the director. If the interview is successful, the poet works with an instructor in a classroom for a six-and-one-half-day residency, after which the poet is assigned a residency of his or her own.

Because of budget cuts and the length of the current waiting list, acceptance in PITS remains largely restricted to poets. If the writer in question, however, happens to work in other genres, he or she is sometimes allowed to teach in that genre, whether it be in play writing, fiction, or nonfiction.

Publications

Every residency is expected to culminate with the publication of an anthology of the student's work, which is edited by the poet-resident and published by the participating school.

THE SCRIPT DEVELOPMENT WORKSHOP
c/o Trent Gough
G.P.O. Box 1846
New York, NY 10116
(212) 489-9520
582-8847

The Script Development Workshop is a nonprofit repertory group of theater, film, and TV professionals, actors and directors, working with writers to develop scripts under the artistic direction of Trent Gough. This is the Workshop's fifteenth year.

The Workshop divides its year into four twelve-week terms. Each workshop enrolls approximately twenty-five writers, twelve actors, twelve actresses, and six directors.

Writers may submit scripts of any length for film, TV, or theater, including musicals. The writer attends rehearsals, leading to a staged reading before Workshop members, followed by a constructive moderated critique. Recent scripts have been on network TV. Writers may also join prime-time TV writing teams or write showcase satirical sketches for production.

Also, for one session a term, top agents are invited to discuss how to get scripts into the marketplace.

People interested must submit applications for membership to the above address. Applicants are then interviewed before they are accepted.

Fees

The current rates are twelve weeks for $80; the entire year is $165.

For further information about applications, rates, and schedules, call the membership secretary, or leave a message for Trent Gough at (212) 489-9521. Or write to the above address.

TEACHERS AND WRITERS COLLABORATIVE
84 Fifth Avenue
New York, NY 10011
(212) 691-6590

The Teachers and Writers Collaborative was founded in 1967 by writers and educators, including the educational theorist Herbert Kohl, to practice and develop methods of teaching creative writing to grade-school children. Writers who have worked with the Collaborative in the past include Muriel Rukeyser, Alan Ziegler, June Jordan, Kenneth Koch, and Philip Lopate. A number of these people have written some of the more influential books on teaching writing in the schools.

In addition to assigning interns and staff members to New York City schools to teach writing, the Collaborative has an ambitious and sizable publication and book distribution program. Books published and distributed by the program include documentations and anthologies of student writing, in addition to guides to teaching methods. A full publication catalog is available free of charge.

Long-term residencies for writers are available in New York City public schools. Many of these residencies are funded by the Urban Corps Program and Federal College Work/Study. The Collaborative also conducts occasional seminars on the teaching of writing.

Publications

Teachers and Writers Magazine is sent to those who are members.

Teachers and Writers Catalogue lists books distributed by Teachers and Writers but not published by them, in addition to books written by Collaborative participants, documents, studies, and anthologies.

Fees

The membership fee is $25. Privileges include a one-year subscription to the magazine, one free copy of a selected Collaborative book, and invitations to seminars.

104

THE WRITERS COMMUNITY, INC.
120 East 84th Street
New York, NY 10028
(212) 348-0160

The Writers Community is a nontuition, nondegree program for persons who will benefit from professional training and from participation in a group that is primarily committed to writing.

One advanced poetry workshop and one advanced fiction workshop, each meeting one evening per week, are offered each semester, in addition to master classes, readings, lectures, and informal discussions. Speakers include writers, critics, and others whose professional experience is of special interest to writers. Attendance at these events is open to workshop members and the public.

To become a member, a writer must submit biographical information and supporting material: a minimum of ten pages of poetry or fifteen to twenty-five pages of prose, depending on the writer's specialty.

Application deadlines are the fifth of January for the spring term and the fifth of September for the fall term. A stamped self-addressed envelope must be enclosed for return of materials.

All workshop participants, past and present, are considered members. No dues are charged, and contributions are voluntary.

Workshops/Readings

Six to eight readings by established writers, invited by the board, are sponsored each year. There are thirteen-week advanced workshops in poetry and fiction, meeting one evening a week, plus individual conference hours.

Writer-in-Residence Program

A resident teaches an advanced poetry or fiction workshop. Residencies are offered to poets and fiction writers who have published at least one full-length book with a commercial, university, or small-press publisher of national importance.

Publications

A newsletter containing announcements, articles, and listings of achievements and activities by members is available without charge to all whose names are on the mailing list.

Fees

Members are asked to contribute $25 or, as an option, an equivalent number of work hours.

7. GRANTS AND FELLOWSHIPS

Change, Inc.

CINTAS Fellowship Program

Creative Artists Public Service Program

National Endowment for the Arts—Literature Program

National Scholarship Research Service

New York State Council on the Arts—Literature Program

The most basic resource for anyone is money. This section includes profiles of the most important city, state, and national grants agencies and also a profile of the organization Change, which offers assistance on a basic level, not for creative work but for short-term aid during emergencies or times of critical financial need. We wish to remind you that most of the service organizations listed in the first part of this book are valuable sources for information about grants and for grants themselves. Extensive information about grants should be researched at the Center for Arts Information and the Foundation Center. There is corporate money, foundation money, as well as government money available for the individual writer.

Teachers and Writers and the Coordinating Council for Literary Magazines are important umbrella organizations that can assist writers and institutions in finding funding. *Coda* and the *Association of Hispanic Artists' Newsletter* are publications for ongoing information about grants, commissions, and opportunities. (See the bibliography for books containing information about obtaining grants.)

CHANGE, INC.
Box 705
Cooper Station
New York, NY 10276
(212) 473-3742

Founded by Robert Rauschenberg, the Change Foundation provides emergency grants to artists of every discipline. These grants range from $100 to $500. Applicants may also receive free medical treatment at facilities that cooperate with Change.

Change's funding comes from a number of public and private sources, art donations, and a variety of fund-raising activities. It is hoped that artists who have received grants from Change in the past will donate artwork or money so that other artists may benefit.

All applications are reviewed by the board of directors, which includes Robert Rauschenberg, James Rosenquist, and Leo Castelli.

The list of situations that Change regards as immediately needy includes medical expenses, utility turn-offs, eviction, fire damage, and any other situation recognized by the board as an emergency during application review.

There are no geographical restrictions and no application deadlines. Applicants must be able to verify their professional status and financial need.

Supporting materials must include a detailed letter describing the financial emergency and why the artist does not have the money to cope with the problem, a professional résumé, reviews of work, and published writing samples, if applicable.

Persons seeking medical treatment from hospitals affiliated with Change should include a letter from their physician.

CINTAS FELLOWSHIP PROGRAM
Cintas Foundation, Inc.
Institute of International Education
809 United Nations Plaza
New York, NY 10017

The Cintas Foundation awards eight fellowships annually in the fields of painting, sculpture, architecture, graphic arts, literature, and music composition to creative artists of Cuban citizenship or lineage. Each fellowship is $5,000.

To be eligible for the award, the Cuban artist must have professional status and be involved in the creative arts, as opposed to the performing arts.

Eligible candidates wishing application forms and additional information should apply to the secretary of Cintas at the above address.

E ARTISTS PUBLIC SERVICE PROGRAM
'th Street, Room 1424
.., NY 10107

(212) 247-6303

The Creative Artists Public Service Program (CAPS) is an independent organization that provides financial support to individual New York State artists in any of twelve disciplines: photography, painting, graphics, mixed media, sculpture, video, film, choreography, fiction, poetry, play writing and screenwriting, and music composition. CAPS arranges with New York State organizations and institutions for community service activities such as workshops, lectures, exhibitions, and performances to be undertaken by its artist fellows.

Since 1982 only six of these twelve disciplines have been funded in one given year; the disciplines are recognized on a rotating basis. Consult CAPS for deadlines and schedules.

Fellowship Program

Eligibility for CAPS fellowships is restricted to permanent residents of New York State who are not currently matriculated in a degree program. Applicants must be able to present a representative body of work and be willing to perform community-related services.

Grants range from an average of $150 for single events to between $3,500 and $10,000 for long-term residencies. Fellowship winners are chosen by panels of professional colleagues in each of the twelve fields. New panels are assembled each year to ensure impartiality.

Artists who win CAPS fellowships work in a number of community environments: schools, libraries, community centers, museums, neighborhood houses, prisons, hospitals, parks, universities, senior citizens' groups, and specialized art centers.

Playwrights' Referral Service (PRS)

This is a lending library of playscripts written by CAPS fellows and writers who have been recommended by the CAPS play-writing panel. The purpose of this library is to bring unproduced playscripts to the attention of producers and directors.

Publications

CAPS Brochure
Annual CAPS Directory of Fellows
Books for purchase (write for list)
Directory of Plays in PRS
CAPS in Capsule (not for sale, reference only)

> "In attempting to be a bridge between the artist and the community, the CAPS program is doing its part to humanize an extremely troubled society. Our very survival as a culture depends on this humanization. What could be more important?"
> —Erica Jong, from preface to *CAPS in Capsule, a Fellowship Program for Artists* (1975).

NATIONAL ENDOWMENT FOR THE ARTS
Literature Program
Regional Representative
2 Columbus Circle
New York, NY 10019

(212) 957-9760

The Literature Program of the National Endowment for the Arts (NEA) provides financial support to writers with strong publishing records and to noncommercial literary magazines and organizations that are committed to excellence and aesthetics in contemporary literature.

The four programs that the NEA Literature Program provides are for individual writers, literary magazines that publish serious contemporary work, audience development, and, occasionally, professional development.

Individual Grants

NEA fellowships to individuals do not exceed $12,500. They are given in the following genres: fiction and creative prose, translation into English, poetry, and script writing. The last two genres will not be funded until 1984.

NEA money is given only to organizations that have noncommercial and tax-exempt status. It is given in the following areas: small-press assistance to literary magazines, distribution projects, and design centers. Design centers are not often funded, but these grants are given for the purpose of improving the typography and design of creative literary publications. The NEA does not give grants to be used as seed money to start small presses; they must have published at least three issues.

Three types of grants are awarded: for writers' residencies, assistance to literary centers, and audience and professional development. The money goes to public institutions for the promotion and dissemination of contemporary literature through readings, performances, exhibits, and shows. Grants to audience-development projects go to such events as book fairs, traveling and permanent exhibits, and other promotional projects.

Grants for professional development go to a few national organizations that provide assistance to writers or sponsor literary programs in ways not defined in the guidelines for audience development.

When reviewing applications for project support, the NEA considers the following factors:

- literary merit of the project
- potential impact of the project
- evidence that the applicant has budgeted appropriately
- general fiscal and organizational responsibility
- completeness and clarity of the application

Nonproject fellowships are reviewed solely on the basis of the literary quality of the manuscript submitted.

NATIONAL SCHOLARSHIP RESEARCH SERVICE
P.O. Box 2516
San Rafael, CA 94912

Toll-free outside California:
(800) 227-1733

Inside California:
(415) 459-3323

Scholarship, fellowship, grant, and loan award information from thousands of private-sector sources can be researched through the staff of the National Scholarship Research Service. Anyone who is attending an accredited school, college, or university and is a United States citizen or a permanent resident, including high school students, undergraduate students, graduate students, and doctoral candidates is eligible to receive information and request a search.

Research is based on biographical information listed on the application. This biographical information includes educational goals, ethnic background, interests, and any data that will make the search appropriate to the individual. Call or write for application and for further information.

Most applicants receive on the average twenty-five to thirty-five possibilities. Research in vocational and technical fields is limited, however.

Fees

There is a $40 processing fee for a search.

NEW YORK STATE COUNCIL ON THE ARTS
Literature Program
80 Centre Street
New York, NY 10013
(212) 587-4537

The Literature Program of the New York State Council on the Arts (NYSCA) supports a wide variety of professional organizations whose activities encourage the creation, publication, distribution, and public appreciation of literature through the genres of poetry, fiction, drama, and nonfiction prose. At the same time that it stresses the development of the public's awareness of the importance of literature, this program provides assistance to individual writers by supporting readings and workshops; by bringing writers into libraries, schools, and other cultural institutions; by building appropriate publication outlets and distribution mechanisms; and by providing workspace for writers. Applications may include, but are not limited to, requests related to audience development, readings, workshops, translation programs, the publication and distribution of magazines and books, conferences, and general support services to the field.

Support is available for administrative and operating expenses and for program costs of organizations that provide a variety of literary programs and services for writers and the general public.

In assessing applications, the Literature Program considers the following:

1. The quality of the literary project being proposed and the need for it

2. The management and fiscal responsibility of the organization

3. The organization's ability to accomplish its goals

Organizations needing advice or assistance in meeting any of these criteria should contact the staff.

Activities supported by the Literature Program that relate to the creation of literature include, but are not limited to, the following:

Workspace

Organizations providing writers time and space to work. Requests may include administrative and operating costs. Organizations should include a detailed description of how the workspace program will operate, how the writers will be selected, and how the program will be publicized.

Workshops

Workshops are led by professional writers giving instruction, guidance, and advice to individuals interested in writing. Priority is given to workshops for professional writers. Requests should include a résumé of the instructor, listing his or her teaching experience, and should give details concerning the location and estimated size of the workshop.

Visiting Writers-in-Residence

The writer is given support and time to work in organizing community programs such as coordinating workshops, holding individual conferences, and giving community readings. Ideally 60 percent of the writer's time is spent writing, while the remaining time is devoted to organizing community programs.

Local sponsoring organizations provide all administrative and promotional services and appropriate space for the writer-in-residence. The application from an organization should include a résumé of the proposed writer, a representative sample of the writer's work, a detailed description of the duties required, and an explanation of the process by which the writer was selected. Only published writers are eligible. Consideration is also given to the writer's previous community experience and to his or her teaching ability. (Note: Funding is available at the maximum rate of $7,500 per six-month period.)

Translation

The Literature Program has undertaken a program to support all phases of translation. Requests from organizations may include support for work in progress, readings by translators, translation workshops, the publication of translations in magazine or book form, and fees to translators for published work.

Support for published work is available for translators who are residents of New York State. Requests from organizations may relate to noncontemporary work that has remained untranslated as well as contemporary works of literature in foreign languages. Preference will be given to work that has received a commitment from a noncommercial publisher. The application from an organization should include a résumé of the proposed translator.

Writers' Appearances

Organizations requesting fees for writers to read or perform in a series may apply directly to the Council on the Arts. Additional support for publicity, promotion, and basic administrative expenses may be included in the request. Attendance, proper promotion, readers in past series, and the audience are all taken into consideration in the evaluation of the application.

Community Programs

The NYSCA Literature Program also provides funding for organizations working to develop an appreciation of literature in different community settings. These organizations may offer programming in a variety of settings, including libraries, schools, and cultural institutions. Priority will be given to groups placing writers in a number of different locations within a community setting.

Literary Magazines

The Literature Program has undertaken a program of direct support for noncommercial literary magazines, which are defined as those magazines that publish a substantial amount of contemporary fiction, poetry, plays, literary criticism, or work in translation. Applicants must obtain detailed supplemental guidelines from the Literature Program before submitting guidelines in this category.

Noncommercial Presses

Support is available for publication and distribution costs to noncommercial publishers that have published at least two volumes of poetry, fiction, drama, or nonfiction prose. Detailed supplemental guidelines are available from the Literature Program to organizations before submitting their applications.

University presses are not eligible for support under this program. It is also unlikely that the Council will offer support to those presses whose editors are primarily engaged in the publication of their own work.

Service Programs to Noncommercial Publishers

Support is available for administrative and general operating expenses for organizations assisting noncommercial publishers by providing prepress and typesetting facilities, by sponsoring book fairs and workshops in design, layout, and distribution, and by producing resource materials for the publishing community.

Distribution

Support is available to noncommercial presses, magazines, and distribution groups that attempt to broaden the reading audience and to increase the sales of books and magazines published in the noncommercial sector.

Application Assistance

If there are any questions about the eligibility of a request or if assistance is needed in filling out the application form, contact:

Literature Program, (212) 587-4537
Fiscal Department, (212) 587-4524

8. WRITERS' CONFERENCES IN THE NORTHEAST

Bennington Writing Workshop

Breadloaf Writers' Conference

Georgetown University Annual Writers' Conference

Green Mountains Writers' Workshops

Hofstra University Summer Writers' Conference

University of Massachusetts Summer Writers Workshop

Rockland Center for the Arts

University of Rochester Writers Workshop

Southampton Writers' Conference

Wesleyan Writers' Conference

Women's Writing Workshops

Workshop in the Illustration and Writing of Children's Books

There are approximately 240 writers' conferences held across the country at which writing on a number of subjects—from cookbooks and history to creative writing and poetry—is discussed. Conferences and workshops can be valuable for a writer who wants more creative help, editorial help, and the opportunity to meet and talk with other writers and possibly meet editors, publishers, and literary agents. Because it is important to be selective, you should carefully review each conference—faculty, style, content, and point of view—in order to determine which is best suited to your interests.

The conferences listed here are primarily in New York State and the Northeast, but a few other well-known symposia have been noted—Georgetown University's conference, for example, which has been meeting for twenty-three years. Each entry includes information on the length of sessions (the majority are held in the latter two weeks of July), faculty who have participated in the past, subjects and genres of the workshops and discussion sessions, fees, and room and board. Deadlines and the opening of sessions tend to change from year to year, and so we encourage the reader to write for more information.

Other sources of information on conferences include the May 1981 issue of *Writer's Digest* (available in most libraries—consult the periodicals index) and, for those in Manhattan, the resource library of Poets & Writers, Inc. (See profile of Poets & Writers, Inc.)

BENNINGTON WRITING WORKSHOP
Bennington College
Bennington, VT 05201

From late June to late July. Sessions last about one month.

BREADLOAF WRITERS' CONFERENCES
Box 500
Middlebury College
Middlebury, VT 05753

Mid to late August. Guest writers have included John Irving, John Gardner, and others.

GEORGETOWN UNIVERSITY ANNUAL WRITERS' CONFERENCE
Writers' Conference, School for Summer and Continuing Education
Georgetown University
Washington, DC 20057
(202) 625-4777

The session in 1982 lasted from July 6 to July 10. Faculty has included poet William Stafford, fiction writer Anne Beattie, and nonfiction writer Joyce Maynard. Genres of instruction: novel, nonfiction, short story, poetry.

Fees

Participation without manuscript, $145; with manuscript, $340. Manuscript criticism is given in afternoon sessions; discussions are held in morning sessions. Additional $95 for academic credit.

GREEN MOUNTAINS WRITERS' WORKSHOPS
College Relations Office
Johnson State College
Johnson, VT 05656

Mid to late July. Workshops and consultations have been given in the past by Hayden Carruth and John Engels.

HOFSTRA UNIVERSITY SUMMER WRITERS' CONFERENCE
Director of Continuing Education, New College
Creative Writing Program
Hofstra University
Hempstead, NY 11550

Two weeks of sessions usually from early July to late July. Workshops in fiction, nonfiction, poetry, TV, screen and play writing, and children's fiction. Past participants have included the late John Gardner, novelist; Bud Schulberg, screen writer and novelist; and poets William Heyen and David Ignatow; and Lila Perl, children's writer. Enrollment fee for credit and noncredit is $350; dormitory an additional $100.

UNIVERSITY OF MASSACHUSETTS SUMMER WRITERS WORKSHOP
Program Coordinator, Writers Workshop
Division of Continuing Education
University Library, South East Entrance
University of Massachusetts
Amherst, MA 01003

Open two weeks in the latter half of July. Sessions are on nonfiction, illustration, cookbook writing, and screenplay writing, in addition to fiction and poetry. Beginning and experienced writers are encouraged to attend. Fees: $95 plus $5 registration fee, housing not included. Room and board is $14 a night single, $19 double.

122

ROCKLAND CENTER FOR THE ARTS
27 Greenbush Road
West Nyack, NY 10994

Sessions in the fall and spring. Programs are multidisciplinary, including literary and the dramatic arts. Courses include journal writing, short fiction, poetry, and creative writing for children. Write for more information.

UNIVERSITY OF ROCHESTER WRITERS WORKSHOP
Coordinator, University of Rochester
Rochester, NY 14627

(716) 275-2342

Conference held in mid-July. No specific requirements to enroll; fee of $160. Workshops are conducted in fiction, nonfiction, poetry, editing, and publishing.

SOUTHAMPTON WRITERS' CONFERENCE
Glen Macleod, Director
Southampton Writers' Conference
c/o English Department
Southampton College
Southampton, NY 11968

Session in 1982 was held from July 19 to 30. Participants have included poets James Merrill and Alan Dugan, novelists John Gardner, Peter Matthieson, and Joyce Carol Oates. Advanced writing workshops by David Bradley, novelist, and Robert Long, poet.

WESLEYAN WRITERS' CONFERENCE
John W. Paton, Executive Secretary
Wesleyan Writers' Conference
Wesleyan University
Middletown, CT 06457

1982 session was July 11 to 16. Participating writers have included Lois Gould, novelist, poets Jean Valentine and Robert Siegel, short story writer Robley Wilson. Besides those on poetry and fiction, workshops have been on children's writing, agents, little magazines, and marketing and editing. Two fellowships for poetry and fiction and several scholarships are available on a competitive basis. Open to students, teachers, and writers, whether published or unpublished. No academic credit. $325 for room, board, and tuition.

WOMEN'S WRITING WORKSHOPS
Program Office
Hartwick College
Oneonta, NY 13820

(607) 274-3143, ext. 361

Sessions are usually from mid or late July to beginning of August. Workshops are in poetry, fiction, play writing, and nonfiction prose. Guest writers have included Marge Piercy, Elaine Gill of the Crossing Press; faculty includes Kirsten Grimstead and Katharyn Machad Aal.

WORKSHOP IN THE ILLUSTRATION AND WRITING OF CHILDREN'S BOOKS
Mrs. Christine Patience
Program Office
Hartwick College
Oneonta, NY 13820

In 1982 sessions were held from August 8 to 21. Guest speakers have included Ariane Dewey, Robert Kraus, and Stephen Roxburgh. Fees: noncredit, $305; $325, credit. Room and board, $154. Deposit of $50 is required.

9. GRADUATE WRITING PROGRAMS

The following is a selected list of graduate writing programs in the United States and Canada. Anyone interested in a particular school mentioned here should write for current information on faculty and course offerings.

Included with addresses is the type of degree offered only when it differs in title from the standard degree in creative writing. For instance, the University of Arkansas offers a Master of Fine Arts in translation as well as an MFA in creative writing. Many Master of Arts programs offer degrees in English with Creative Thesis, or Options, or Emphasis; all of these variations from the standard MA in creative writing are listed.

Graduate creative-writing programs are usually divided between workshop discussions of the students' work and literature seminars requiring term papers and so forth. Other seminars, especially when taught by writing teachers themselves, have looser requirements regarding scholarly writing. Degrees of Creative Writing Emphasis and Options tend more toward the production of scholarly and research papers.

If information on financial aid was available, it is included here; that is, financial aid outside of loans and college work study—teaching assistantships, out-of-state tuition waivers (often attendant on Teaching Assistantships), fellowships, and nonteaching assistantships (usually in research and editing). When appropriate, the abundance and frequency of this financial aid is mentioned.

The difference between the MA and the MFA is in the number of required credit hours; 30 for MAs and 60 for the MFAs. When teaching assistantships are added to the students' academic responsibilities, the time to finish the degree is twice as long, so that an MFA takes four years and an MA takes two.

Since either of the degrees alone supplies weak credentials for teaching, it is advisable to apply at schools that offer teaching assistantships. At these schools students in writing programs instruct large freshman classes in introductory composition. Teacher assistantships are often necessary for students who wish to work as instructors in institutions of higher education.

A useful reference for information on writing programs is *The Associated Writing Programs' Catalogue of Writing Programs,* edited by Kathy Walton. It is available for $5 from the Associated Writing Programs. (See profile on page 97.)

MFA PROGRAMS IN THE UNITED STATES AND CANADA

UNIVERSITY OF ALABAMA: Director, Writing Program, Department of English, University, AL 35486. Teaching assistantships with stipends ranging from $3,700 to $4,700 that include tuition waiver. Also teaching/writing fellowships ($2,350 per semester), stipend of $1,850 per year for editorship of *Black Warrior Review,* and graduate council fellowships with no teaching requirements.

UNIVERSITY OF ALASKA: Writing Program Director, Department of English, Fairbanks, AK 99701.

UNIVERSITY OF ARIZONA: Creative Writing Program, Department of English, Tucson, AZ 85721. Graduate assistantships with out-of-state tuition waiver; limited number of nonresident scholarships.

UNIVERSITY OF ARKANSAS: For information on MFA in Creative Writing, write to the Program in Creative Writing, Department of English, Fayetteville, AR 72701. For MFA in Translation, write to Miller Williams, Department of English. Teaching assistantships for most incoming students.

BOWLING GREEN STATE UNIVERSITY: BFA, MFA, and Ph.D. in writing, with creative dissertation. Write to Director, Creative Writing Program, Department of English, Bowling Green, OH 43403. Financial aid, four fellowships awarded. Other financial aid: teaching assistantships, fellowships, work study.

UNIVERSITY OF BRITISH COLUMBIA: Write to Douglas Bankson, Head, Department of Creative Writing, UBC, 2075 Westbrook Place, Vancouver, British Columbia V6T 1W5, Canada. (Include self-addressed stamped envelope with Canadian stamps of International Reply Coupons with all submissions.)

BROOKLYN COLLEGE, CITY UNIVERSITY OF NEW YORK: Jack Gelber, Director. Writing Program, Department of English, Brooklyn, NY 11210. MFA in play writing, poetry, and fiction. MFA in creative writing, 36 semester hours. No data on financial aid. Urban Corps and work-study available.

UNIVERSITY OF CALIFORNIA AT IRVINE: Director, The Program in Writing, Department of English and Comparative Literature, Irvine, CA 92717. Associateships and teaching assistantships available; some tuition waivers for out-of-state applicants; some research assistantships for minority students available.

COLUMBIA UNIVERSITY: Daniel Halpern, Chairman, The Writing Division, School of the Arts, New York, NY 10027. MFA is awarded. About 25 percent of the students receive fellowships covering less than half of annual tuition; financial awards are the Tennessee Williams Prize and the Simon & Schuster fellowship. Only recently instituted, these fellowships are awarded to one student each year. No teaching assistantships; other financial aid such as work-study and Urban Corps.

CORNELL UNIVERSITY: James McConkey, Writing Program Director, Department of English, Ithaca, NY 14853.

EASTERN WASHINGTON UNIVERSITY: John Keeble, Coordinator, Creative Writing Program, English Department, Cheney, WA 99004. Financial aid: teaching fellowships and work-study assistantships. Fellows and assistants from out-of-state pay in-state fees. One fellowship is offered annually for managing editor of *Willow Springs* magazine.

EMERSON COLLEGE: Director, Writing Program, 148 Beacon Street, Boston, MA 02116. MFA in creative writing was approved for 1980—1981. Regularly offers courses in scriptwriting and comedy. Write for more information.

GEORGE MASON UNIVERSITY: Director, Writing Program, Department of English, Fairfax, VA 22030. MFA in English with special concentration in writing. Financial aid: internships, graduate assistantships in teaching, tutorial work, and research.

GODDARD COLLEGE WRITING PROGRAM AT VERMONT COLLEGE: Roger Weingarten, MFA Writing Program, Box 510, Vermont College, Montpelier, VT 05602. MFA in creative writing. A nonresidential program with twelve-day residencies, followed by six-month writing projects. Student submits work to "field faculty" every three weeks. No financial aid except loans.

INDIANA UNIVERSITY: Creative Writing Committee, Department of English, Bloomington, IN 47401. A new program, begun in the fall of 1980. Financial Aid: six associate instructorships ($2,665 a year for teaching undergraduate creative writing courses each semester); $1,000 Ernest Hemingway Fellowship in Writing.

UNIVERSITY OF IOWA: Director, Writers' Workshop, Iowa City, IA 52242. Besides MFA programs in fiction and poetry, criticism in the arts program was begun in 1980–1981. Financial aid: Graduate College tuition scholarships and research assistantships ($2,350 per year); graduate teaching assistantships in Liberal Arts College ($3,750 per year); teaching-writing fellowships ($5,404 per year); three fellowships for criticism in the arts program.

UNIVERSITY OF MASSACHUSETTS: Director, MFA Program in English, 452 Bartlett Hall, Amherst, MA 01003. MFA in English; 24 credits in literature; twenty-four workshops. Financial aid: fellowships including tuition waivers awarded to ten first-year students; teaching assistantships available to second- and third-year students; includes tuition waivers.

UNIVERSITY OF MONTANA: Chairman of Graduate Committee, Department of English, Missoula, MT 59801. MFA in drama, poetry, and fiction. Financial aid: work-study; nonresident fee waivers.

UNIVERSITY OF NORTH CAROLINA, GREENSBORO: Writing Program Coordinator, Department of English, Greensboro, NC 27412. Randall Jarrell Fellowship of $1,000 in conjunction with assistantship to outstanding first-year student. Also research assistantships; some out-of-state tuition waivers.

UNIVERSITY OF OREGON: Director of the Writing Program, Department of English, Eugene, OR 97403. Five to six teaching assistantships are available each year for second-year MFA students.

SARAH LAWRENCE COLLEGE: Administrative Director, Graduate Studies Program, Bronxville, NY 10708. MFA in writing. Very limited amount of financial aid.

WICHITA STATE UNIVERSITY: Coordinator of Creative Writing, Department of English, Box 14, Wichita, KS 67208. Most students receive teaching assistantships in addition to partial remission of tuition and fees.

MA WRITING PROGRAMS IN THE UNITED STATES AND CANADA

UNIVERSITY OF ALBERTA: Chairman, Department of English, Edmonton, Alberta, T6G 2E5 Canada. MA in English with creative thesis.

ANTIOCH UNIVERSITY: Dean, Antioch International, Yellow Springs, OH 45387. Program held in London and at Oxford in the summer. Several partial fellowships available.

ARIZONA STATE UNIVERSITY: Director, Writing Program, Department of English, Tempe, AZ 85281. Teaching assistantships.

UNIVERSITY OF BALTIMORE: Writing Program Director, Department of English, Baltimore, Maryland 21201. MA in publications design. Competitive scholarships and graduate assistantships.

BEMIDJI STATE UNIVERSITY: Department of English, Bemidji, Minnesota 56601. MA in English-Education with creative dissertation. Teaching assistantships.

BOSTON UNIVERSITY: Secretary, Creative Writing Program, 256 Bay State Road, Boston, MA 02215. Fellowships, teaching assistantships.

BRIGHAM YOUNG UNIVERSITY: Chairman, Writing Committee, Department of English, Provo, UT 84602. MA with creative thesis. Sixty assistantships.

BROWN UNIVERSITY: Director, Department of English, Providence, RI 02912. MA in creative writing.

CALIFORNIA STATE UNIVERSITY, CHICO: Writing Program Coordinator, Department of English, Chico, CA 95929. MA in English with creative dissertation.

CALIFORNIA STATE UNIVERSITY, HAYWARD: Writing Program Director, Department of English, Hayward, CA 94542.

CALIFORNIA STATE UNIVERSITY, LONG BEACH: c/o Department of English, Long Beach, CA 90840. MA in English with creative option.

CALIFORNIA STATE UNIVERSITY, SACRAMENTO: Creative Writing Committee Chairman, Department of English, Sacramento, CA 95819. MA in English with creative writing concentration and creative thesis.

UNIVERSITY OF CALIFORNIA, DAVIS: Graduate Advisor, Department of English, Davis, CA 95616. Teaching assistantships for second-year students; two teaching assistantships for exceptional first-year students.

CARNEGIE-MELLON UNIVERSITY: Writing Program Director, Department of English, Pittsburgh, PA 15213. MA in professional writing; for writing in government and industry.

CASE WESTERN RESERVE UNIVERSITY: Chairman, Department of English, Cleveland, OH 44106. MA in English with creative dissertation. Teaching assistantships.

CENTRAL MICHIGAN UNIVERSITY: Writing Program Director, Department of English, Mt. Pleasant, MI 48853. Limited number of teaching assistantships and fellowships.

CENTRAL STATE UNIVERSITY: Director, Department of Creative Studies, Edmond, OK 73034. MA in English with creative writing major. Thesis may be TV or film scripts.

CITY COLLEGE OF NEW YORK, CITY UNIVERSITY OF NEW YORK: Directors, Creative Writing Program, 138th Street and Convent Avenue, New York, NY 10031. MA in creative writing to a selected number of students; no more than fifty enrolled per year. $3,000 De Jur Award in Creative Writing; also limited number of fellowships.

COLORADO STATE UNIVERSITY: Chairman, Creative Writing Department, Department of English, Denver, CO 80210. MA in English with creative thesis. Teaching assistantships, fellowships, and a limited number of scholarships available.

DRAKE UNIVERSITY: Chairman, Department of English, Des Moines, IA 50311. MA in English with creative thesis.

UNIVERSITY OF EVANSVILLE: Chairman, Department of English, Evansville, IN 47701. MA in continuing studies with concentration in creative writing.

FAIRLEIGH DICKINSON UNIVERSITY: Writing Program Director, Department of English, Fordham-Madison Campus, Madison, NJ 07940. MA in English with creative or professional writing thesis.

FLORIDA STATE UNIVERSITY: Chairman, Department of English, Tallahassee, FL 32306. MA in English with writing emphasis.

UNIVERSITY OF FLORIDA: Department of English, Gainesville, FL 32601. MA in English with emphasis on creative writing. Teaching assistantships.

GEORGE MASON UNIVERSITY: Director of Writing Program, Department of English, Fairfax, VA 22030. MA in English with concentration on professional writing and editing; MA in English with concentration in writing of fiction or poetry; MA in English with special concentration in creative writing. Internships, teaching assistantships, tutorial work, and research.

UNIVERSITY OF GEORGIA: Director, Writing Program, Department of English, Athens, GA 30602. MA in English with creative thesis.

GODDARD WRITING PROGRAM AT VERMONT COLLEGE: Plainfield, VT 05667. MA in writing, nonresident program. Written work is sent by student to core faculty, supplemented by intensive residencies lasting twelve days.

UNIVERSITY OF HAWAII: Director, Creative Writing Program, Department of English, 1733 Donagho Road, Manoa, Honolulu, HI 96822.

HOLLINS COLLEGE: Program Director, Department of English, Hollins College, VA 24020. MA in film and theater; MA in English, creative writing, contemporary literature, and literary criticism.

UNIVERSITY OF HOUSTON: Program Director, Creative Writing, Department of English, Houston, TX 77004. MA in English and creative writing with creative thesis.

UNIVERSITY OF ILLINOIS, CHICAGO CIRCLE: Chairman, Program for Writers, Chicago, IL 60680. MA in English with specialization in creative writing. Teaching assistantships, fellowships.

INDIANA STATE UNIVERSITY: Coordinator of Creative Writing, Terre Haute, IN 47809. MA in English with creative thesis.

INDIANA UNIVERSITY: Creative Writing Committee, Bloomington, IN 47401. MA in English with a concentration in creative writing. Annual Ernest Hemingway Fellowship of $1,000.

JOHNS HOPKINS UNIVERSITY: Coordinator, The Writing Seminars, Baltimore, MD 21218. MA in writing. Seminars. Teaching fellowships to half of a class of 30.

KANSAS STATE UNIVERSITY: Writing Program, Department of English, Manhattan, KS 66506. MA in English with creative report. Majority of students have teaching assistantships.

UNIVERSITY OF KANSAS: Director of Graduate Writing Program, Department of English, Lawrence, KS 66045. MA in English with creative writing option.

UNIVERSITY OF LOUISVILLE: Director, Creative Writing Program, Louisville, Kentucky 40208. MA in English with creative thesis. Teaching assistantships, scholarships, service assistantships, editorial assistantships, and fellowships.

MIAMI UNIVERSITY: Program Director, Department of English, Oxford, Ohio 45056. MA with creative writing concentration.

MICHIGAN STATE UNIVERSITY: Writing Program Director, Department of English, East Lansing, Michigan 48824. MA in English with creative dissertation. Limited number of teaching assistantships.

UNIVERSITY OF MICHIGAN: Chairman, Department of English, Ann Arbor, Michigan 48109. Hosts visiting writers, but offers no creative degree proper. Hopwood Award for creative writing.

UNIVERSITY OF MISSOURI, COLUMBIA: Director, Creative Writing Program, Department of English, Columbia, Missouri 65211. MA in English and creative writing. Fellowships, teaching assistantships, and grants.

UNIVERSITY OF MISSOURI, KANSAS CITY: Chairman, Department of English, Kansas City, MO 64110. Teaching assistantships.

MURRAY STATE UNIVERSITY: Writing Program Director, Department of English, Murray, KY 42071. MA in English with emphasis in creative writing. Eight graduate assistantships.

UNIVERSITY OF NEBRASKA, LINCOLN: Chairman, Department of English, Lincoln, NE 68588. MA in English with creative writing option.

UNIVERSITY OF NEW BRUNSWICK: Department of English, P.O. Box 4400, Fredericton, New Brunswick E3B 5A3, Canada.

UNIVERSITY OF NEW HAMPSHIRE: Director, MA in writing program, Hamilton Smith Hall, Durham, NH 03824. Graduate assistantships and other financial assistance.

NEW MEXICO STATE UNIVERSITY: Director, Writing Program, Department of English, Las Cruces, NM 88003. MA in English with creative writing emphasis.

UNIVERSITY OF NEW MEXICO: Director of Creative Writing, Department of English, Albuquerque, NM 87131. Teaching assistantships, tuition waiver, for teaching.

NEW YORK UNIVERSITY: Chairman, Department of English, New York, NY 10003. MA in English with concentration in creative writing. Some teaching assistantships, a few fellowships, and scholarship aid.

UNIVERSITY OF NORTH DAKOTA: Chairman, Department of English, Grand Forks, ND 58202. MA in English with creative thesis option.

OHIO STATE UNIVERSITY: Writing Program Director, Department of English, Columbus, OH 43210

OHIO UNIVERSITY: Director of Creative Writing, Department of English, Athens, OH 45701. MA in English with creative thesis.

OKLAHOMA STATE UNIVERSITY: Chairman, Department of English, Stillwater, OK 74074. MA in English with creative writing emphasis and thesis. Teaching assistantships and nonteaching assistantships.

OLD DOMINION UNIVERSITY: Chairman, Department of English, Norfolk, VA 23508. MA in English with writing emphasis.

UNIVERSITY OF OREGON: Director, Writing Program, Department of English, Eugene, OR 97403. MA in English with creative dissertation.

UNIVERSITY OF PITTSBURGH: Director of Graduate Studies, Department of English, Pittsburgh, PA 15260. MA in English and writing. Teaching assistantships.

QUEENS COLLEGE, CITY UNIVERSITY OF NEW YORK: Writing Program Director, Department of English, Flushing, NY 11367. MA in English (creative writing).

SAM HOUSTON STATE UNIVERSITY: Writing Program Director, Huntsville, TX 77340. MA with option of creative thesis. Teaching assistantships, editorial assistantships.

SAN DIEGO STATE UNIVERSITY: Writing Program Director, Department of English, San Diego, CA 92182. MA in English with emphasis in creative writing. Teaching assistantships on competitive basis, and other scholarships.

SAN FRANCISCO STATE UNIVERSITY: Secretary, Creative Writing Department, 1600 Holloway Avenue, San Francisco, CA 94132. MA in English with concentration in creative writing. No teaching assistantships.

UNIVERSITY OF SOUTH ALABAMA: Creative Writing Program, Department of English, Mobile, AL 36688. MA in English with creative dissertation. Three nonteaching assistantships to graduate students.

SOUTHERN CONNECTICUT STATE COLLEGE: Writing Program Director, Department of English, New Haven, CT 06515. MA/MS with a concentration in creative writing; degree for high school teachers.

SOUTHERN METHODIST UNIVERSITY: Director of Writing Program, Department of English, Dallas, TX 75275. MA in English with creative dissertation.

UNIVERSITY OF SOUTHERN MISSISSIPPI: Director, Center for Writers, Hattiesburg, MS 39401. MA in English with creative writing emphasis. Stipends of $4,000 for MA students on a competitive basis.

SOUTHWEST TEXAS STATE UNIVERSITY: Writing Program Director, Department of English, San Marcos, TX 78666. MA in English with creative thesis.

UNIVERSITY OF SOUTHWESTERN LOUISIANA: Director, Creative Writing Program, Department of English. MA in English with creative writing option. Teaching assistantships and a limited number of fellowships.

STANFORD UNIVERSITY: Director, Creative Writing, Stanford, CA 94305. MA in English/creative writing. Three academic scholarships offered each year. Six Wallace E. Stegner Writing Fellowships carrying a stipend of $5,000 each; four are fiction, two are poetry.

STATE UNIVERSITY OF NEW YORK, ALBANY: Director of Graduate Study, Department of English, HU 335, SUNY-Albany, 1400 Washington Avenue, Albany, NY 12222. MA in English—writing sequence. $3,700 fellowships for beginning MA students, $4,400 teaching fellowships for more advanced students, $5,000 presidential fellowships. All fellowships carry full tuition waiver.

STATE UNIVERSITY OF NEW YORK, BINGHAMTON: Writing Program Director, Department of English, Binghamton, NY 13901. MA with certificate in creative writing.

STATE UNIVERSITY COLLEGE OF NEW YORK, BROCKPORT: Chairman of the Graduate Committee, Brockport, NY 14420. MA in English with creative dissertation. Several graduate assistantships.

SYRACUSE UNIVERSITY: Director of Writing Program, Department of English, Syracuse, NY 13210. MA in English with creative thesis option. Teaching assistantships, four creative writing fellowships. In addition, one university fellowship.

UNIVERSITY OF TEXAS, AUSTIN: Chairman, Department of English, Austin, TX 78712. MA in English with concentration in creative writing. Two university scholarships.

UNIVERSITY OF TEXAS, DALLAS: Director, Translation Center, Box 688, Richardson, TX 75080. MA in humanities with a concentration in writing and tranlsation. Teaching and research assistantships.

UNIVERSITY OF TEXAS, EL PASO: Writing Program Director, Department of English, El Paso, TX 79968. MA in English with creative writing option. Teaching assistantships available on a competitive basis, graduate school fellowships, awards include the remission of out-of-state tuition.

TRINITY UNIVERSITY: Writing Program Director, Department of English, San Antonio, TX 78284. MA in English with emphasis in creative writing.

UNIVERSITY OF TULSA: Graduate Faculty of Modern Letters, 600 South College Avenue, Tulsa, OK 74104. MA in modern letters with emphasis in rhetoric and writing.

UNIVERSITY OF UTAH: Director of Creative Writing, Department of English, Salt Lake City, UT 84112. Ph.D. in English with creative writing emphasis. Teaching assistantships and full fee/tuition waivers.

UNIVERSITY OF VIRGINIA: Writing Program Director, Department of English, Charlottesville, VA 22903. MA with emphasis in creative writing. Six Hoyns Fellowships of approximately $4,000 each were awarded for the academic year of 1981–1982.

WASHINGTON UNIVERSITY: The Writers' Program, Box 1122, St. Louis, MO 63130. MA in writing. Scholarships: $4,750 in the form of tuition remission or university fellowships ($4,750 tuition remission plus a stipend of up to $3,000 for the first year).

UNIVERSITY OF WASHINGTON: Writing Program Director, Department of English, Padelford Hall/GN#30, Seattle, WA 98195. MA in English with concentration in creative writing. Teaching assistantships pay $582 per month. Readerships for literature classes offer $250 per quarter. The Loren D. Millman Scholarship offers $3,000.

WAYNE STATE UNIVERSITY: Writing Program Director, Department of English, Detroit, MI 48202. MA in English with creative thesis (or creative essay, a shorter creative work).

WEST VIRGINIA UNIVERSITY: Chairman, Department of English, Morgantown, WV 26506. MA in English with creative thesis option.

WESTERN WASHINGTON UNIVERSITY: Director of Creative Writing, Department of English, Bellingham, WA 98225. MA in English with creative writing concentration. Teaching assistantships and work/study appointments on a competitive basis.

WICHITA STATE UNIVERSITY: Coordinator of Creative Writing, Department of English, Box 14, Wichita, KS 67208. MFA in creative writing. Teaching assistantships, partial remission of tuition and fees.

UNIVERSITY OF WINDSOR: Department of English, Windsor, Ontario N9B 3P4, Canada. MA in English Literature and creative writing. Graduate financial assistance up to $6,400 is available.

UNIVERSITY OF WISCONSIN, MILWAUKEE: Coordinator of the Creative Writing Program, Department of English, Milwaukee, WI 53201. MA in English with creative writing emphasis.

UNIVERSITY OF WYOMING: Head, Department of English, Laramie, WY 82071. MA in English with concentration in creative writing. Teaching assistantships available.

10. WRITERS' COLONIES AND WRITERS' ROOMS

WRITERS' COLONIES

Artists for the Environment

Dobie-Paisano Fellowship

Dorland Mountain Colony

Carla Eugster

Fine Arts Work Center in Provincetown, Inc.

William Flanagan Memorial Center for Creative Persons / The Edward Albee Foundation, Inc.

The Hambridge Center for Creative Arts and Sciences

D. H. Lawrence Summer Fellowship

The MacDowell Colony

Millay Colony for the Arts, Inc.

The Ossabaw Island Project

Ragdale

Virginia Center for the Creative Arts

Helene Wurlitzer Foundation of New Mexico

Yaddo

WRITERS' ROOMS

Frederick Lewis Allen Memorial Room

Snug Harbor Cultural Center

The Writers' Room, Inc.

Writers' Studio / Mercantile Library

Writers Colonies

There are about eighteen colonies in the United States that regularly admit writers into their residencies. Some are rather selective, like Yaddo and the MacDowell Colony; others appear willing to accept young and promising writers. Note that the best time to apply for residencies at any of these places is winter, when there is the least demand—at least in the northern United States.

The information listed here follows this order: name of colony, addressee's title, length of residency, fees, supporting materials, and financial aid, if available. Descriptions of the facilities are terse; these details are given whenever possible.

Another source of information on colonies is an article from *Coda,* the newsletter of Poets & Writers, Inc. In their May–June 1978 issue, they describe most of the colonies we mention. Since then, the article, "Fifteen Havens for Writers," has been updated and is available in reprint from Poets and Writers for $1 plus postage. The Foundation Center and Center for Arts Information are other reliable sources of information on colonies, conferences, and grants. (See profile of the Foundation Center on page 89.)

ARTISTS FOR THE ENVIRONMENT
Star Route, Box 14
Columbia, NJ 07832
(201) 581-2237   Contact: Joel Levy, Director

This Foundation offers artist-in-residence programs for the National Park Service in the Delaware Water Gap. They are particularly concerned with young artists. Lodging is provided, and artists are granted a small stipend. A residency can last up to three months.

DOBIE-PAISANO FELLOWSHIP
University of Texas at Austin
Main Building 101
Austin, TX 78712

Address inquiries to the director. The program is open only to artists who are Texans. Consult the above address or Poets & Writers, Inc., from which this address was obtained.

DORLAND MOUNTAIN COLONY
Box 6
Temecula, CA 92390
(213) 798-8315

Address all inquiries to project coordinator.

The Dorland Mountain Colony is located on a nature sanctuary of three hundred acres. This is the only colony west of the Rocky Mountains. Residencies are from one to three months. Facilities are provided without charge. Some stipends are available.

CARLA EUGSTER
P.O. Box 41
Woodville, VA 22749
(703) 987-8913

There are residencies year-round, with a minimum of one week at a cost of $45. There are no application deadlines.

FINE ARTS WORK CENTER IN PROVINCETOWN, INC.
24 Pearl Street
Provincetown, MA 02657
(617) 487-9960

The Fine Arts Work Center provides studios and living accommo-
dations for ten writers and ten visual artists from October through
April. Stipends and fellowships are available. The artists are selected
by an impartial jury, and although registered students are not eligible,
the emphasis is on younger artists of demonstrated talent. It has an
international reputation and attracts many visiting luminaries. Application forms and samples of work are required by February 1.

WILLIAM FLANAGAN MEMORIAL CENTER FOR CREATIVE
PERSONS/THE EDWARD ALBEE FOUNDATION, INC.
14 Harrison Street
New York, NY 10003
(212) 221-3319

The location of the residencies is in Montauk, New York. The Center
functions mainly for playwrights and writers, although some facilities
are available to visual artists. Six artists at a time are housed free from
June to October for approximately four weeks. Letters of intent and
recommendations, along with slides or a project proposal, should be
sent as soon as possible. Please enclose a self-addressed stamped envelope for the return of materials.

THE HAMBRIDGE CENTER FOR CREATIVE ARTS
AND SCIENCES
P.O. Box 33
Rabun Gap, GA 30568   Contact: Mary Creely Nikas,
(404) 746-5718 or 746-2491   Executive Director

The Hambridge Center, on Betty's Creek in the highlands of Georgia,
offers workshops and seminars on the arts, handcrafts, and nature.
It is a cultural focus for the community and holds lectures, exhibitions, and concerts. It operates a residency program from mid-April
to mid-October which provides, at modest cost, a studio/cottage for
the use of artists and natural scientists. Résumés and samples of work
should be received by the end of February. Three to four works of
supporting materials exemplifying the writer's development should be
included along with the application.

140

D. H. LAWRENCE SUMMER FELLOWSHIP
Department of English
Humanities Building, Room 217
University of New Mexico
Albuquerque, NM 87106
(505) 277-6340   **Contact: Director**

The University of New Mexico honors D. H. Lawrence by providing a $700 stipend and free residence for the summer at Lawrence's ranch near Taos. The residency is not limited to writers. Applicants should send their résumés, samples of work, and letters of recommendation from September to January.

THE MacDOWELL COLONY
145 West 58th Street 12C
New York, NY 10019
(212) 757-1432

Also: Peterborough, NH 03458   **Contact: Nancy Englander,**
(603) 924-3886   **General Director**

The MacDowell Colony is a well-established and well-known artists', retreat. MacDowell can accommodate more than thirty artists at one time. Most stay for two months, and each has an individual and isolated studio. Many artists return as often as they can. Meals are provided. The cost is approximately $10 per day, although fellowships are available based on one's ability to pay. Application forms, supportive materials, and letters of recommendation are required. Deadlines are mid-January (for summer session), mid-April (fall), mid-July (winter), and mid-October (spring). Samples of work should be included along with applications.

MILLAY COLONY FOR THE ARTS
Steepletop, Austerlitz, NY 12017
(518) 392-3103   **Contact: Project Director**

This is the former estate of Edna St. Vincent Millay. The estate is open all year. During the summer five residencies of one month are offered; in the winter, there are three residencies of two months. There is no application deadline, and no financial aid is offered. There are no residence fees, but contributions are welcome.

THE OSSABAW ISLAND PROJECT
The Ossabaw Foundation
P.O. Box 13397   **Contact: Geoffrey Movius,**
Savannah, GA 31406   **Executive Director**

The Ossabaw Island Foundation provides a working retreat on one of Georgia's "golden barrier" islands. Ossabaw is an island wildlife and plant refuge. Residencies last from one to six weeks for people in the arts, sciences, and humanities. Ten visual artists, writers, scholars, and scientists are housed and fed for up to two months at $50 per week. Facilities also include an experimental, interdisciplinary, independent study program and a number of research projects conducted by universities.

The season is from October to June, and some scholarships are available. There is no deadline for application. Residents must be nominated by the Project's advisory board or by a former resident of the colony.

RAGDALE
Ragdale Foundation
1230 North Green Bay Road
Lake Forest, IL 60045
(312) 234-0366   **Contact: Alice Ryerson**

Ragdale is especially hospitable to writers. Situated on one of the few undisturbed pieces of prairie left in Illinois, it maintains a rare tranquility. Ragdale is open from October to June. The foundation houses and feeds three artists at a time and provides two separate studios at a rate of $70 a week. Some financial aid is available.

Supporting materials, including samples of poetry, prose, and excerpts of longer works, should be included along with applications.

VIRGINIA CENTER FOR THE CREATIVE ARTS
Box VCCA
Mt. San Angelo,
Sweet Briar, VA 24595   **Contact: Administrative Assistant**

There are twelve year-round residencies open to writers on the Mt. San Angelo estate adjacent to Sweet Briar College. Admission is selective. Supporting materials and samples of work should be sent for consideration. The actual cost of the residency is $50 per day, and residents are asked to pay as much of this as they can. The VCCA suggests at least $15 a day.

HELENE WURLITZER FOUNDATION OF NEW MEXICO
Box 545
Taos, NM 87571
(505) 758-2413   **Contact: Executive Director**

The Helene Wurlitzer Foundation is open all year and offers residencies of usually three months to twelve artists. Rent for the studio apartments is free, but residents must pay for food and living expenses. No monetary grants are made. Creative ("not interpretive") artists working in all media are accepted. Application forms with samples of work, references, and a project proposal are required. There is no deadline for applications.

YADDO
Box 395, Union Avenue
Saratoga Springs, NY 12866
(518) 584-0746

Contact: Curtis Harnack,
Executive Director

Yaddo has served as an artists' retreat for more than fifty years. Up to twenty-five artists live in the mansion and use studios scattered around the grounds of the Trask Estate. Visual artists, composers, and writers are welcome. Admission is selective, and samples of work are required. Previous recipients in its history have included William Carlos Williams, Robert Lowell, and Aaron Copeland. The summer season lasts from May to October, in which there are twenty-one to twenty-five residencies from one to two months. In the winter there are eight to nine.

The deadline for filing applications is March 1. Applications must be requested before February 15 of the year prior to the residency period requested.

Note: Addresses and information on four of the artists' colonies listed in the preceding pages were found in an article printed in *Coda: Poets & Writers Newsletter,* June/July 1978, volume 5, number 5, Copyright 1978, Poets & Writers, Inc.

These colonies are Dobie-Paisano, Carla Eugster, William Flanagan/Edward Albee Foundation, and the Dorland Mountain Colony.

Writers' Rooms

One of the most important resources in any city for any artist or writer is "a room of one's own." We have described here four rooms for writers. We hope that this kind of information becomes a model for what writers can look for in any community.

FREDERICK LEWIS ALLEN MEMORIAL ROOM
Creative Director
The Research Libraries
The New York Public Library
New York, NY 10018

This working space was established with a grant form the Ford Foundation as a tribute to Frederick Lewis Allen, the author of *Only Yesterday,* the popular account of the 1920s. The F.L.A. Memorial Room is loaned to writers for one year without charge so that they may finish their book projects. Admission is limited to writers who are currently working under a book contract. Applications for admission must be accompanied by a photocopy of the book's contract. Even with this prerequisite, applications exceed the number of people that it is possible to admit. Applicants who cannot be granted their requests are placed on a waiting list. They are informed of their status within two weeks.

Applications may be received from the address given above.

SNUG HARBOR CULTURAL CENTER
914 Richmond Terrace
Staten Island, NY 10301
(212) 448-2500

Located on an eighty-acre historic park, Snug Harbor is a performing and visual arts center with art galleries, shops, restaurants, rehearsal space, and meeting rooms. The Center rents workspace to artists of all disciplines, including writers.

Located five minutes from the Staten Island ferry and forty-five minutes from Manhattan, Snug Harbor is an ideal retreat for a writer who needs workspace. According to one of its staff, "It's like being in the country, but you're only an hour from Manhattan."

Writers interested in renting workspace should call the above number. The Center also rents space for seminars, conferences, and readings. Rentals are not restricted to Staten Island residents. Artists, however, who do rent workspace must be of professional and recognized status.

THE WRITERS ROOM, INC.
1466 Broadway
New York, NY 10036
(212) 289-2537

Recently relocated in the Knickerbocker Building at Broadway and Forty-second Street, the Writers Room provides working space for up to thirty-six writers. Nominal fees are charged for its use, and facilities include a kitchen, a bathroom, a storage area for typewriters and files, and a small reference library. Desks are screened off from each other, and writers have access to this space day and night, seven days a week.

Any writer who can demonstrate a serious commitment to a literary project is eligible for admission. The most characteristic resident of the Writers Room is a writer who is working on either a first or a second book. Since the board of directors wishes to promote diversity among the writers who use the room at the same time, creative as well as nonfiction writers are welcome to apply.

Fees for the use of the room for each three-month period range from $80 to $125, depending on the extent to which the writer will use the room.

WRITERS' STUDIO/MERCANTILE LIBRARY
17 East 47th Street
New York, NY 10017
(212) 755-6710

The Mercantile Library has been in existence since 1820 as a private membership institution which has been called "a club for book lovers." Its 185,000 volumes are primarily fiction, biography, travel, and history. A special nineteenth-century collection amounts to another 55,000 volumes. Use of the library requires an annual membership fee of $45. Members receive a library card and the annual membership newsletter.

The Library has recently added a new service: the Writers' Studio, a space available to writers on a renewable three-month basis for up to a year at the cost of $100 for each three-month period. There are fourteen spaces, three of which are reserved for writers of children's books.

Unpublished authors who can demonstrate serious intent are welcome to apply. Applications can be obtained at the Mercantile Library or by writing to the above address.

11. SMALL PRESSES AND MAGAZINES

Selected list of small presses and magazines in the New York area

Selected list of special-interest small presses and magazines

List of small-press distributors and bookstores

Committee of Small Magazine Editors and Publishers (COSMEP) profile

> "I think the time is not far off when 99 percent of literary writers will first appear in noncommercial or small-press publications and will find their audience in them."
> —Frank Conroy, Director
> NEA Literature Program, 1982

The small-press movement is one of the most encouraging phenomena for writers, especially here in New York City. It has been estimated that there were more than three hundred small presses in the Lower East Side alone in 1982. The growth of small presses has been attributed to the growing need to publish work that otherwise would not find a publisher. Each year, as the conglomerates buy up the traditional companies, the rationale behind publishing books is not always good work, but profit. So the need to print and distribute new, interesting written works in a less commercial fashion is imperative.

Small press means anything from elaborate, well-bound books to photocopies stapled together. Each of the small presses has its own point of view. The criteria for our selection of general interest presses include duration of existence, proximity to New York City, accessibility to new writers, and aesthetic preference. What all the small presses have in common is this problem: distributing their works and getting the books to the readers. We have included a list of distributors and bookstores where small presses, artists' books, and magazines can be found.

Here's some practical advice for submitting manuscripts to a magazine or small press.

- Before you send out a manuscript, carefully research where to send it. Be aware of the kind of work the press publishes. Use your library and bookstores to look over the variety of publications. Use the *International Directory of Little Magazines and Small Presses* and the *Literary Marketplace,* which have valuable information. It is a waste of time and effort to submit work to publications that do not print your kind of work.

- To get an idea of the range of work of a publisher, write for a catalog. Always include a self-addressed, stamped envelope.

- Write to the publisher for guidelines for submission. Remember to include a self-addressed, stamped envelope.

- Send manuscripts to the acquisitions editor; use the name of the current editor *only* if you are sure of it.

- Work must be clearly typed and neat.

- It is not necessary to send a cover letter.

- Some publications welcome unsolicited work and some do not. Be sure to find out.

General-Interest Small Presses and Magazines in the New York Area

AMERICAN BOOK REVIEW
John Tytell, Rochelle Ratner, Editors
P.O. Box 188
Cooper Station
New York, NY 10003

Founded in 1977, this magazine is devoted entirely to reviews written by creative writers as opposed to professional reviewers. Unsolicited reviews are encouraged, preferably by writers themselves, although most reviews are assigned. The *American Book Review* prefers critical writing that departs from the standard review form and favors reviews of books published by small presses. Bimonthly; $1 for a single copy. Annual subscription price is $6.

ANTAEUS/ECCO PRESS
Daniel Halpern, Charlotte Holmes, Editors
18 West 30th Street
New York, NY 10001

Antaeus is a quarterly that has published poetry, fiction, interviews, novel excerpts, and long poems since 1970. Contributors in the past have included Louise Gluck, James Merrill, Robert Hass, Italo Calvino, Edmund White, William Harrison, and William Kotzwinkle. The price of a single copy depends on size—usually $6. *Ecco Press* began in 1974 with the publication of the *American Poetry Series,* which includes the work of James Tate, Louise Gluck, Robert Hass, and Sandra MacPherson. The press also reprints collections of John Logan, John Ashbery, and W. S. Graham. Books are distributed by W. W. Norton and Company, Inc.

ASSEMBLING PRESS
Scott Helms, David Cole, and Richard Kostelanetz, Compilers
(See Future Press.)
P.O. Box 1967
Brooklyn, NY 11202

Founded in 1970, *Assembling Press* is committed to avant-garde printed art and literary forms in which the distinction between the two forms is erased. Examples include concrete poetry, books as objects, and typographical art. One issue a year at $4.95.

149

CHELSEA MAGAZINE
Sonia Raiziss, Editor
P.O. Box 5880
Grand Central Station
New York, NY 10163

Published since 1958, Chelsea purports to have no special biases and deliberately maintains an eclectic editorial policy. Contributors to recent issues include Fernando Arrabal, Thomas A. Disch, Paul Bowles, Gerard Malanga, Howard Moss, Susan Sontag, and Jonathan Williams. One to two issues a year at $4 a copy; annual subscription rate is $7.

FULL COURT PRESS, INC.
Ron Padgett, Joan Simon, and Anne Waldman, Editors and Publishers
15 Laight Street
New York, NY 10013

Publishers of books since 1974. Books by Frank O'Hara (*Selected Plays),* Larry Fagin, and Allen Ginsberg (*Harmonium Blues).* Two of its principals, Ron Padgett and Anne Waldman, are closely associated with the St. Mark's Poetry Project and share with the Project a preference for nonliterary language and poetry that can be performed and for the work of the French surrealists. The average price of books is $6 a copy. Write for complete list of publications.

FUTURE PRESS
Richard Kostelanetz, Editor
(See also *Assembling Press*)
P.O. Box 73
Canal Street Station
New York, NY 10013

Publishing since 1976, *Future Press* has an emphasis similar to *Assembling,* with a commitment to avant-garde printed art, such as concrete poetry, visual novels, and alternative book forms. Write for publications list.

HANGING LOOSE PRESS, AND HANGING LOOSE (Journal)
Robert Hershon, Dick Lourie, Ron Schreiber, Denise Levertov, and Emmett Jarrett, Contributing Editors
231 Wyckoff Street
Brooklyn, NY 11217

Published since 1966. Unsolicited manuscripts welcome; *Hanging Loose* takes an active interest in new writers. Past contributors include Harvey Elliot, Helen Adam, and Rochelle Ratner. Three issues per year: $2.50 per copy. Annual subscription of $5.50 per year.

NEW YORK QUARTERLY
William Packard, Editor
P.O. Box 2415
Grand Central Station
New York, NY 10017

Published since 1969, *New York Quarterly* regularly publishes poems and interviews and limited amounts of fiction. Great pains are taken to make unbiased selections of unpublished manuscripts. $3 per copy; subscription for four issues is $11.

PARIS REVIEW
George A. Plimpton, Editor
45-39 171 Place
Flushing, NY 11358

The *Paris Review* has published poetry, fiction, articles, and interviews since 1952. Renowned for its contribution to contemporary writing and for its interview series with such authors as Evelyn Waugh, William Carlos Williams, and Ezra Pound. $3.50 per copy; annual subscription for four issues is $11.

PARNASSUS: POETRY IN REVIEW
Herbert Leibowitz, Publisher
205 West 89th Street
New York, NY 10024

Since 1972 *Parnassus* has published interviews and reviews of poetry exclusively. Some of its past contributors include Adrienne Rich, Guy Davenport, and Hayden Carruth. Published twice a year at $6 per copy; annual subscription rate is $12.

PULPSMITH
The Generalist Association, Inc.
Harry Smith, Sidney Bernard, Tom Tolnay, Editors
5 Beekman Street
New York, NY 10038

Published as the *Smith* since 1964; as of 1981, however, revised its format to *Pulpsmith,* which is a digest as opposed to a literary magazine. No longer regarding its criteria as strictly "literary," *Pulpsmith* publishes science fiction, mystery, fantasy, lyrics and ballads, as well as poetry and creative fiction. *Pulpsmith* welcomes unsolicited material. A single copy is $2; samples are $1.50 each; an annual subscription is $8.

SUN PRESS AND SUN MAGAZINE
Bill Zavatsky, Editor and Publisher
347 West 39th Street, Apt. 7N
New York, NY 10027

Originally published as *Sundial* in 1966, *Sun Press* has been publishing books and its magazine since 1975. Past contributors have included John Ashbery, Philip Lopate, Ron Padgett, and Harvey Shapiro. The magazine does not accept unsolicited material. *Sun Books* include translations of the prose poems of Max Jacob, Malcolm de Chazal (*Sense Plastique),* and reissues of poems by James Schuyler. Other poets include Michael O'Brien, Paul Violi, and Ron Padgett.

UNMUZZLED OX (MAGAZINE)
Michael Andre, Editor and Publisher
105 Hudson Street, #311
New York, NY 10013

Since 1971 the magazine has published fiction, poetry, photos, artwork, criticism, and interviews. Recent contributors include Robert Creeley, Gregory Corso, Daniel Berrigan, and Eleanor Antin. Published up to four times a year; $5 per copy.

Note: This information was found in the *International Directory of Little Magazines and Small Presses,* edited by Lem Fullam (Paradise, CA: Dustbooks, Inc., softcover, $13.95).

Special-Interest Small Presses and Magazines

Arts Publico Press (*Revista Chicano-Requena*)
Nicholas Kanello
University of Houston
Houston, TX 77004
(713) 749-4721

Revista Chicano-Requena is a journal of Hispanic literature and art that publishes poetry, fiction, art, photos, literary criticism, and articles on folklore and popular culture.

Bridge: Asian American Perspectives
Renee Tajima, Managing Editor
32 East Broadway
New York, NY 10002
(212) 925-8685

This is a quarterly magazine published by Asian Cine-vision that is entering its eleventh year. Range: poetry and fiction, as well as Asian and American issues. Mainly through subscriptions. Write for submission guidelines.

Asian American Studies Center
Russell Leong, Editor
3232 Campbell Hall
University of California
Los Angeles, CA 90024
(213) 824-2974

Publishes scholarly essays, book reviews, short stories, poetry. Some issues focus on Asian-American literature.

EAST WIND MAGAZINE
East Wind Politics and Culture of Asians in America
Eddie Wong, Editor
P.O. Box 26229
San Francisco, CA 91426

Publishes articles, poetry, and short stories having to do with the experience of Asians in this country. Articles of topical interest, such as housing in the United States, are published. Interested in new writers. Has a specific cultural section of poetry and short stories and features.

There is a New York City local committee working to promote the magazine and its concept. For further information contact Sasha Hobri at (212) 689-3475.

The Feminist Press
Florence Howe, Editor
P.O. Box 334
Old Westbury, NY 11568

Nonprofit, tax-exempt publishing house. Reprints neglected writings by women, biographies, children's books, and materials for nonsexist curricula at every educational level.

Greenfield Review Press
Joseph and Carol Bruchac
R.D. 1
P.O. Box 80
Greenfield Center, NY 12833
(518) 584-1728

Poetry and reviews. Open to both new and established poets. Some past issues have included prison writing, modern African poetry, and American Indian writing. Some recently published books include poetry by Kofi Awoonor, Kofi Anyidoho, and Kwesi Breuo. The length of books published ranges from small chapbooks of twenty-four pages to full-size volumes. Because the press is often backlogged, it is best to inquire before sending a manuscript.

Logbridge
Rhodes, Inc.
Frank Graziano, Editor
P.O. Box 3254
Durango, CO 81301

Publishes poetry, long poems, and translations of contemporary foreign authors. Queries are always welcome. Unsolicited manuscripts will be returned unread. Most recent publications: *A World Rich in Anniversaries,* prose poems by Jean Follain, translated by Mary Feeney and William Matthews, and *Canisy,* prose by Jean Follain, translated by Louise Guiney.

Lollipop Power, Inc.
P.O. Box 1171
Chapel Hill, NC 27514
(919) 929-4857

Fiction. Publishes nonsexist, nonracist books for children. Priority is given to manuscripts with strong female protagonists, especially black, native American, and Latino.

Maize Press **(MAIZE: Notebooks of Xicano Art and Literature)**
Alurista, Yelina
Box 8251
San Diego, CA 92102
(714) 235-6135

Poetry, fiction, art, photos, cartoons, satire, criticism, excerpts from novels, long poems, plays, interviews. Chicano, Indian, Latin American preferences.

Montana Council for Indian Education
Hap Gilliland
P. O. Box 31215
Billings, MT 59107
(406) 252-7475

Publishes small books on themes related to American Indian life and culture, both fiction and nonfiction.

The National Association of Third World Writers
373 Fifth Avenue Suite 1007
New York, NY 10016

Since September 1982, the Association has been compiling a list of publishers, presses, periodicals, bookstores, and distributors that are committed to working with the literature of third world writers. Send inquiries to Gale Jackson at the above address.

Persephone Press, Inc.
The Lesbian Writers' Quarterly
Gloria Greenfield, Treasurer
P.O. Boxz 7222
Watertown, MA 02172
(617) 924-0336

Fiction, nonfiction, art, photos. Primary goal is printing books on women's spirituality. Published *The Coming Out Stories* (1980). a book of personal histories that has importance to many lesbians.

Review, **Center for Inter-American Relations**
680 Park Avenue
New York, NY 10021

A journal that publishes Latin American literature in translation as well as reviews, critical materials, essays. Considers unsolicited reviews or translations. 1,500 words. Submissions should be sent to the editor. Enclose a self-addressed stamped envelope for the return of materials.

SCANDINAVIAN REVIEW
Kate Daniels, Richard Jones
Open Studio
127 East 73rd Street
New York, NY 10021
(212) 879-9779

Poetry, fiction, articles, art photos, interviews, satires, criticism, plays. Focus is on contemporary American-Scandinavian culture and society. Suggested length of articles is 2,000 words. Enclose a self-addressed stamped envelope.

SEZ, A Multi-Racial Journal of Poetry & People's Culture
Shadow Press, U.S.A.
Jim Dochniak, Editor
P.O. Box 8803
Minneapolis, MN 55408
(612) 823-1319

Poetry, fiction, articles, art, photos, cartoons, interviews. Special attention is given to third world writers as well as writers whose work reflects ethnic and/or class consciousness. Each issue is divided into thematic sections: Please inquire or suggest themes. No "art for art's sake." *Sez* is interested in publishing writers who are dealing with social issues and working for a more humane society. Unsolicited manuscripts are welcome. Enclose a self-addressed stamped envelope and a short biographical sketch. Length should be 2,500 words for prose and ten pages maximum for poetry.

Spinsters, Inc.
Maureen Brady
R.D. 1
Argyle, NY 12809
(518) 854-3109

Publishes only feminist fiction, articles, criticism, nonfiction. Recent authors include Audre Lorde and Lynn Strongin.

SUN & MOON PRESS
Douglas Messerli, Howard N. Fox
4330 Hartwick Road, #418
College Park, MD 20740
(301) 864-6921

Publishes short books of poetry, fiction, art, and critical theory. Interest is in texts that experiment with or are grounded in language theory and/or that stress style. Recent publications include *Shade* by Charles Bernstein, *Who's Listening Out There?* by David Antin, and *Oracle Night* by Michael Bronstein.

Sunbury (A Poetry Magazine)
Sunberry Press
Virginia Scott
P.O. Box 274
Jerome Avenue Station
Bronx, NY 10468

Publishes work by women, working-class, and third-world poets, including Fay Chiang, Marge Piercy, Quincy Troup, and Lorraine Sutton.

13th Moon Inc.
Ellen Marie Bissert, Editor
Inwood Station
New York, NY 10034
(212) 569-7614

Poetry, fiction, articles, art, photos, interviews, criticism, reviews, collages, plays, nonfiction. Publishes quality work by women. Particularly interested in lesbian and feminist writing and third-world and working-class perspectives.

UNICORN: A Miscellaneous Journal
Karen Rokow, Editor
P.O. Box 118
Salisbury, VT 05749
(802) 352-4263

Articles, cartoons, interviews, satire, criticism, reviews, letters, collages, art, nonfiction. *Unicorn* publishes offbeat and humorous aspects of popular culture and folklore, literature, gardening, progressive education, children's literature. Manuscripts must be mailed first-class because they will have to be forwarded to editor during the winter.

Wood Ibis
Place of Herons Press
James Cody, Editor
P.O. Box 1952
Austin, TX 78767
(512) 442-6917

Poetry, fiction, articles, art, criticism, excerpts from novels, photos, cartoons, interviews, reviews, long poems, and plays. "Emphasis on the revival of the ceremonial in the passage of seasons, of the earth and life; sense of place; of the vision quest; encouraging tribalism. Respect for nature and animals. No distinction between primitive and civilized." Focuses on the ongoing community through literature, third world, women, Chicano, blacks, ecology, North America, Latin America, Celtic, European, tribal culture, and language/literature. Distributes some Native American titles for *Unicorn Books* and *Greenfield*.

Small Press and Magazine Distributors

Following is a sampling of distributors and bookstores where small presses, artists' books, and magazines can be found.

The Book Bus
c/o Visual Studies Workshop
31 Prince Street
Rochester, NY 14607

Founded in 1974. 100 percent literary or visual art publications. Distribution limited to the Northeast. Individual sales. Book bus and bookstore. Nonprofit, grant supported.

Bookpeople
2940 Seventh Street
Berkeley, CA 94710

Founded in 1968. 85 percent small press. National distribution but sales representatives on West Coast only. Individual sales at the Berkeley warehouse. No magazines. Write for free book catalog.

Bookslinger
P.O. Box 16251
2163 Ford Parkway
St. Paul, MN 55116

Founded in 1979. 95 percent literary small press. Distribution nationwide but sales representative concentrates on Midwest. Nonprofit, grant assisted. Write for free book catalog.

Casa Editorial
2707 Folsom Street
San Francisco, CA 94110

Founded in 1976. Emphasis on Latin American publications. Individual sales. Bookstore. Nonprofit, grant assisted.

Con-Berry
451 Bowling Green
New York, NY 10004

Write for free book catalogs.

The distributors
702 South Michigan
South Bend, IN 46618

Founded in 1972. All paperback, 25 percent small press but not all literature. Distribution nationwide. No sales to individuals.

Gnomon Distribution
P.O. Box 106
Frankfort, KY 40401

Founded in 1977. 100 percent literary, very selective (15 presses). Distribution nationwide. No individual sales. No magazines.

Gotham Book Mart
Ms. Janet Morgan
Small Press Department
41 West 47th Street
New York, NY 10036

Write for free book catalog.

New England Small Press Association (NESPA)
45 Hillcrest Place
Amherst, MA 01002

Founded in 1974. 100 percent small press, members only. Distribution limited to Northeast. Individual sales. Nonprofit, grant supported.

New York State Small Press Association (NYSPA)
P.O. Box 1264
Radio City Station
New York, NY 10019

Founded in 1975. 100 percent small press, members only. Distribution mainly in New York State. Individual sales. Nonprofit, grant supported. Write for free book catalog.

Plains Distribution Service
P.O. Box 3112, Room 406, Block 6
620 Main Street
Fargo, ND 58102

Founded in 1975. 100 percent literary, almost all small press. Emphasis on Midwest authors or content. Distribution in Midwest only. Individual sales. Book bus. Nonprofit, grant supported.

Printed Matter, Inc.
7 Lispenard Street
New York, NY 10013

Founded in 1976. 100 percent books by artists, some one-of-a-kind. Bookstore, individual sales. Nonprofit, grant supported. Catalog available for $4.

St. Luke's Book Distributor
Suite 401, Mid-Memphis Tower
1407 Union Avenue
Memphis, TN 38104

Founded in 1974. 100 percent small press. Emphasis on mid-South presses or content. Distribution nationwide.

SBD (formerly Serendipity)
1636 Ocean View Avenue
Kensington, CA 94707

Founded in 1969. 100 percent literary small press, member-based but now distributing to some nonmembers. Distribution nationwide. Books only. Individual sales. Nonprofit, grant assisted.

Small Press Traffic
2841B 24th Street
San Francisco, CA 94114

Founded in 1974. 100 percent literary small press. Will take any literary title. Individual sales. Bookstore. Nonprofit, grant supported.

Segue Foundation
300 Bowery
New York, NY 10012

The Segue Foundation is a nonprofit organization that serves as an umbrella group to receive grants for twenty to twenty-five smaller art groups. The Foundation also distributes small-press poetry books directly from publisher to local bookstores. Segue publishes its own books and broadsides and large, posterlike copies of poems. Write for free book catalog.

Spring Church Book Company
P.O. Box 127
Spring Church, PA 15686

Founded in 1974. Not a distributor in the strict sense, but a retail mail-order bookseller. 100 percent poetry, from small, university, or commercial publishers. All individual sales. No magazines.

Subterranean Company
Box 10233
Eugene, OR 97440

Write for free book catalogs.

Swift Lizard Distributors
Box A, New Mexico Tech
Socorro, NM 87801

Founded in 1979. 90 percent literary small press. Nonprofit, grant supported.

This list was taken from the *Philadelphia City Paper,* September 1982, and an issue of *Coda,* the Poets & Writers newsletter.

COMMITTEE OF SMALL MAGAZINE EDITORS AND PUBLISHERS (COSMEP)
P.O. Box 703
San Francisco, CA 94101

Although not a New York–based organization, COSMEP is an association of small-press publishers throughout the United States, and so it merits an investigation by any prospective small-press publisher. As a nonprofit, tax-exempt association of small-press publishers, it provides helpful information to its members on distribution and marketing. In cooperation with Dustbooks, it rents mailing lists, and its monthly newsletter features articles full of practical advice to small presses—from how to approach arts agencies to advice on distributing books. COSMEP regularly holds conferences of its regional membership and exhibits the publications of its members at annual American Library Association and American Booksellers Association conventions.

Support Services Alliance (SSA)

Members of COSMEP automatically become members of SSA, an affiliated but independent organization that grants to its members a number of benefits concomitant with those offered by COSMEP. SSA benefits include legal inquiry, group-rate insurance, and pricing/purchasing services.

Publications

COSMEP Newsletter, published monthly, is available to members only. It contains national news of members' publications and services offered by other organizations, such as distribution and mailing lists, and prints reports from regional conferences and articles on the business of small and large press publishing.

Fees

Membership is $40 a year and is open to any small press or periodical, including those still in the planning stages.

12. READINGS: LIVE AND RECORDED

The American Poetry Archives

The Giorno Poetry Systems Institute, Inc.

Manhattan Theatre Club

New Wilderness Foundation

New York City Poetry Calendar

The Poetry Project Tape Collection at St. Mark's Church

The Village Voice/"Spoken Words"

The Villager

There are more poetry readings in New York City each night than there are in most cities in a week or a month or a year. It is estimated that there are between two hundred and three hundred writers and poets living and writing in the area from Chelsea to City Hall alone. And more and more we are beginning to identify the many writers, artists, and programs outside the Manhattan area in their different ethnic and cultural entities. We are learning that poets and writers want to speak, to read, to share their works with audiences. Readings happen every night in churches, cafés, community centers, in artists' lofts, art galleries—in Manhattan, Queens, the Bronx, Brooklyn, and Staten Island.

We have included some basic information on readings around New York City. It is up to you to search out information about readings in your own neighborhood. Consult your local and borough newspapers, community newsletters, and neighborhood community centers for listings of readings to attend or for opportunities to read.

Some organizations keep archives of recorded poetry readings: The American Poetry Archives, The Giorno Poetry Systems Institute, The New Wilderness Foundation, and The Poetry Project. Information on these groups is included here also.

THE GIORNO POETRY SYSTEMS INSTITUTE, INC.
222 Bowery
New York, NY 10012
(212) 925-6372

The Giorno Poetry Systems Institute is an international nonprofit, tax-exempt organization founded in 1968 to sponsor and develop projects involved with increasing the communication of poetry between poet and audience. Using technology and media as the means to investigate the possibilities, the result has been an ongoing changing series of projects.

Dial-A-Poem in New York and at other installations around the country used telecommunications in 1968 for the first time to extend the telephone to a mass audience, with thousands of people listening to a poet read a poem. The Dial-A-Poem Poets LPs, with twenty records produced so far in the series, are widely distributed and are played on FM radio stations around the country.

The Giorno Poetry Systems Institute is constantly working on developing new formats for the radio production of poetry: Satellite Poetry, the Poetry Experiment on WBAI, Radio Free Poetry, and WPAX. The Institute has also developed productions of many theatrical events, including poets performing with musicians, dancers, and theater companies.

During the last fifteen years, more than 150 poets have appeared in the various productions representing a broad range of traditions from all over the United States—young and unknown, established greats, historic poetry readings, experiments in sound poetry and performance. All minorities—women, gays, blacks, and Hispanics—are included in publications and presentations.

Records of many of the performances are available. Call for further information on poetry events and festivals.

THE AMERICAN POETRY ARCHIVES*
Poetry Center
San Francisco State University
Science Building, Room 154
1600 Holloway
San Francisco, CA 94132
(415) 469-1056 or 469-2227

For twenty-seven years the Poetry Center has sought to introduce West Coast audiences to the works of both established and little-known poets and writers by sponsoring readings, courses, and discussions. The Center has also brought poetry to the young with the Poets in the Schools program and programs for the elderly.

The Poetry Center has established an American Poetry Archive that contains more videotapes and audiotapes than the Library of Congress. The Center began making the audiotapes in 1954 and the videotapes in 1973. This important program developed from the concern that the oral tradition of poetry was being lost and that future generations would miss the opportunity to hear poems interpreted by their authors.

Tapes are widely distributed. Hundreds of secondary schools and colleges in all the states as well as Japan, Canada, and France have borrowed them. Prices for leasing the tapes range from $15 to $30 per showing. Videotapes are half-inch reel-to-reel and three-quarter-inch cassettes. Many tapes are in color. A catalog is available for $3 describing the 400 tapes in the archive, with a full-page description of each and a biographical sketch of the writer.

Every time a tape is shown, the writer or poet receives $5.50. Call or write for more information.

*Although the American Poetry Archives is in San Francisco, not New York City, it has been included here because it houses one of the largest collections of poetry tapes in the country, and New York City writers (as well as writers everywhere) may be interested in using this service.

MANHATTAN THEATRE CLUB
321 East 73rd Street
New York, NY 10021
(212) 288-2500

A professional theater that produces about ten shows a year. They select submitted plays and musicals and develop and refine them with the playwrights.

In addition to staged readings and various special events, they produce *Writers in Performance,* a regular series of poetry readings. This series schedules ten events a year in a variety of formats. There are readings given by poets and fiction writers and readings conceived around a single theme. In the past there have been readings by Peter Matthieson and staged readings of works by Colette and S. J. Perelman.

Interested writers may submit unsolicited manuscripts to the Director of the Writers in Performance Series at the above address. The deadline is September 15 of each year.

The Manhattan Theatre Club maintains an internship program in the literary department that is open to students and nonstudents alike. Positions are nonsalaried.

Each year one resident is hired on a nonsalaried basis by the literary department to help as an administrative assistant and researcher.

NEW WILDERNESS FOUNDATION
326 Spring Street, Room 208
New York, NY 10013
(212) 807-7944

New Wilderness maintains an archive of music and sound poetry and also publishes cassettes of experimental and traditional sound work.

New Wilderness Audiographics/Audiocassette Series is an ongoing series of published cassettes* of experimental and traditional poetry, music, drama, and storytelling. Works include American Indian spiritual songs, New Guinea music, Bread and Puppet Theater, new music and language works by Alison Knowles, Donna Henes, Tom Johnson, Philip Corner, Jackson MacLow, Annea Lockwood, and a host of other artists. The poet Julia Lebentritt has been collecting lullabies in ethnic communities for a new release, entitled "New York City Lullabies."

New Wilderness Listening Room, curated by ethnomusicologist/composer Barbara Benary, is a listening facility for public access to the music archives of New Wilderness and other organizations with related artistic focus. The Listening Room's central focus is the New York City experimental music community. It also includes text/sound, poetry, world music (Amerindian), storytelling, and materials from international and interethnic sources that blend old traditions with new and maintain a connection with nature. Call 807-7944 for an appointment.

---

*Each cassette is $8.50 plus tax. At present there are thirty-six cassettes in the series. For a list of Audiographics, write to the above address. See profile in Chapter 1 for complete information about this organization.

NEW YORK CITY POETRY CALENDAR
397 1st Street
Brooklyn, NY 11215
(212) 475-7110

The New York City Poetry Calendar provides a complete monthly listing of all poetry events in New York City. It is distributed free to bookstores, libraries, and community centers and is available by mail ($8/year) from 13 East 3rd Street, New York, NY 10003. To list your reading or workshop, write the Brooklyn address given above by the fifteenth of the preceding month. The calendar has a monthly readership of 4,000.

THE POETRY PROJECT TAPE COLLECTION
St. Mark's Church
Second Avenue and 10th Street
New York, NY 10003
(212) 674-0910

Since 1966 the Poetry Project has been regularly taping readings, performances, workshops, and lectures. The Collection has more than 420 tapes, which are catalogued and indexed.

The free catalog listing these tapes can be obtained by calling or writing to the above address. The tapes are not for sale, but anyone may hear particular readings by appointment. Copies can be made for individuals, at cost, but only with written permission from the poet in question.

It is hoped that the Poetry Project will be able to establish a more permanent archive of this unique collection. Bob Holman, the director, welcomes help from individuals interested in establishing this project.

THE VILLAGE VOICE/"Spoken Words"
Voice Literary Supplement
842 Broadway
New York, NY 10003
Contact: Judy Hottensen

Each month *The Village Voice* publishes a literary supplement in which the "Spoken Words" column lists readings throughout the month at different poetry centers (the New School, the West Side YMCA, Jefferson Market Library, and so on). Listings should be sent to Judy Hottensen by the fifteenth of the month.

THE VILLAGER
88 Seventh Avenue South
New York, NY 10014
(212) 982-7200

The Villager is a weekly newspaper of Lower Manhattan and features cultural information and reports on events happening below Thirtieth Street. It contains listings of poetry readings and workshops for writers, film, music, art, theater, and dance.

The newspaper will list any appropriate event occurring in Lower Manhattan. The deadline is two weeks prior to the event.

The *Villager* also prints a complete listing of theater performances and reviews and features yearly awards for outstanding achievement in downtown theaters.

The Villager can be purchased at local sellers and by subscription.

Here is a list of organizations offering *reading opportunities*. See individual profiles for more information.

Academy of American Poets

American Indian Community House Gallery

Association of Hispanic Arts

Basement Workshop, Inc.

Bronx Council on the Arts

Brooklyn Arts and Culture Association

Center for Inter-American Relations

Dramatists Guild

Greek Cultural Center

El Grupo Morivivi, Inc.

Foundation for the Community of Artists

The New Wilderness Foundation

PEN American Center

Poetry Center of the 92nd Street Y

The Poetry Project of St. Mark's Church

Poetry Society of America

Poets & Writers, Inc.

Queens Council on the Arts

Staten Island Council on the Arts

Theatre Communications/TCG Dramatist Sourcebook

Women's Salon

Appendixes

Special Issues in Developing a Writing Career

Advice from an Agent
Here is practical advice on a writing career from an agent. We also encourage you to read *Literary Agents: A Complete Guide,* available from Poets & Writers, Inc. (See profile on page 36.)

Gloria Loomis, Watkins-Loomis Agency

First and foremost, a person should possess a great deal of drive and optimism to pursue a writing career. There will be constant blocks to getting published, since editorial decisions are so subjective. A writer should not take rejection personally—he or she will need a strong ego.

My advice to those still trying to develop their writing skills is to find a good writing course. If you have a good teacher, you'll learn a lot and may perhaps gain contacts that will help your career. A writing course also provides a nurturing, supportive atmosphere in which to discuss your work. I have found in many cases that it has helped writers take themselves more seriously.

Once you've started your project, you need an agent to get a foot in the door. Editors are less willing to take the time to read work by new writers today, given the state of the economy. But if a proposal from an unknown comes with an endorsement from a reputable agent, editors are more likely to read it. Of course, there are always the isolated instances of unagented individuals having their manuscripts read, published, and becoming best sellers, but these cases are extremely rare.

To find an agent, I suggest you submit your material to new agents or associates of larger agencies. Most established agents are too busy to take on new clients. Young agents, on the other hand, are hungrier and looking for new projects to promote. To find addresses and numbers of agents, look in the *Literary Market Place* (published by Bowker).

A writer should submit a synopsis and a few chapters of his or her work to an agent. Although this work should be in final form, agents are usually willing to work with skilled writers to develop a manuscript. When an agent believes that a manuscript is ready for submission to publishing houses, he or she sends it to different editors, trying to match the work with the editor's interests.

I work differently with different writers, because everyone has different needs—some are independent and some need more nurturing. Basically, though, I see myself as a facilitator between publisher and writer. I do not believe in the idea that some writers have of finding a powerful agent who will protect them. I don't see myself in that role, and I don't get along with writers who have such needs.

If a writer is to succeed with or without an agent, he or she must be willing to work hard—first producing the work, then deciding where to submit it. For instance, a writer should learn which small presses are out there and the type of work that they want. Then, if a writer is without an agent, he or she should submit work to these small presses, since they are more likely to publish new writers.

I firmly believe that publishing still is a meritocracy—success is based on talent, not on whom you know. However, this doesn't mean you should isolate yourself. Networking with young agents, editors, and other writers is important.

The Business of Being a Writer—the Marketplace

Sometimes it is helpful for a writer to think of himself or herself as a small business, and in order to conduct this small business (or large business) profitably, a writer needs information. There are many courses, workshops, and seminars on business and legal matters that are being conducted at universities and colleges. There are various service organizations—some quite specific ones such as Volunteer Lawyers for the Arts and the Accountants for the Public Interest—that can help writers, and there are many specialized books on the subject. (See profiles of these organizations and bibliography.)

We are including here a copy of a schedule for an excellent and inclusive sixteen-week series that was held at Just Above Midtown/Downtown in 1982 to give you an overview of the important issues you should be thinking about and the names of people who can provide you with some of the answers. This particular series was held in a space downtown, not thought of as a "writers'" space, that is the kind of creative use of resources for which you should be looking.

Cheri Fein, free-lance writer, poet, and fiction writer, coordinated the Business of Being a Writer Series under a writer-in-residence grant from the New York State Council on the Arts.

WRITING FOR A LIVING I: FREELANCING FOR MAGAZINES AND NEWSPAPERS

November 9   Panel Discussion

JANET CHAN Articles Editor, Glamour
JANE CIABATTARI Fiction writer; Managing Editor, Redbook
CYNTHIA CROSSEN Managing Editor, The Village Voice
LINDA GUTSTEIN Fiction writer; freelance writer; former Senior Editor, Woman's World
ROBIN STRAUS Vice President, Wallace & Sheil Literary Agency

FREELANCING FOR MAGAZINES AND NEWSPAPERS

November 16   Free Workshop

WRITING FOR A LIVING II: COMMERCIAL WORK

November 23   Panel Discussion

TIM DLUGOS Poet; journalist; direct mail copywriter and consultant
FREDERICK FEIRSTEIN Poet; playwright; TV, radio, and documentary scriptwriter
SHELBY HEARON Novelist; collaborator on Barbara Jordon's autobiography
GREGORY KOLOVAKOS Translator; ghostwriter; Literature Program Director, N.Y. State Council on the Arts
JOE LeSEUR Fiction writer; scriptwriter for soap operas

COMMERCIAL WRITING

November 30   Free Workshop

COPYRIGHT, CONTRACTS, AND TAXES

December 7   Discussion

ROBERT CARR C.P.A.; partner, Lutz & Carr
JERRY SIMON CHASEN Publishing and entertainment attorney, Linden & Deutsch

PUBLISHING POETRY AND FICTION IN MAGAZINES

December 14   Panel Discussion

PETER GLASSGOLD Co-editor, New Directions in Prose and Poetry
JAMES GWYNNE Editor, Steppingstones
MIMI JONES Associate Fiction Editor, Redbook
JENNIFER MOYER Poet; Executive Director, Coordinating Council of Literary Magazines
HALLIE GAY WALDEN Managing Editor, The Paris Review
ALAN ZIEGLER Poet; fiction writer; Editor, Some Magazine

PUBLISHING POETRY AND FICTION IN MAGAZINES

December 21   Free Workshop

FURTHERING YOUR FORMAL EDUCATION: GRADUATE PROGRAMS, WORKSHOPS, AND CONFERENCES

January 11   Panel Discussion

LAUREL BLOSSOM Poet; Director, The Writers Community
RICHARD PRICE Novelist; graduate of and teacher at Columbia University Writing Program; has taught at Yale, SUNY Binghamton, SUNY Stony Brook, NYU
MARK RUDMAN Poet; graduate of Columbia University Writing Program; has taught at Queens College, Manhattan Community College, Teachers & Writers Collaborative, N.Y. State Poets-in-the-Schools
GARLAND LEE THOMPSON Playwright; Founding Director, Frank Silvera Writers' Workshop

ALAN ZIEGLER Poet; fiction writer; graduate of City College Writing Program; teaches at Columbia University; has taught at Teachers & Writers Collaborative and N.Y. State Poets-in-the-Schools

LITERARY AGENTS AND REPRESENTATIVES

January 18   Panel Discussion

JERRY SIMON CHASEN Publishing and entertainment attorney, Linden & Deutsch
CONNIE CLAUSEN President, Connie Clausen Associates
RUSSELL GALEN Literary agent, Scott Meredith Literary Agency
GLORIA LOOMIS President, Watkins-Loomis Agency
LYNN SELIGMAN Literary agent, Julian Bach Literary Agency
ROBIN STRAUS Vice President, Wallace & Sheil Literary Agency

LITERARY AGENTS AND REPRESENTATIVES

January 25   Free Workshop

GETTING HELP: GRANTS, AWARDS, COLONIES, SERVICE ORGANIZATIONS, AND FRIENDS

February 1   Panel Discussion

FAY CHIANG Director, Basement Workshop
HENRI COLE Interim Director, The Academy of American Poets
ELLIOT FIGMAN Executive Director, Poets & Writers, Inc.
CURTIS HARNACK Executive Director, Yaddo Artists Colony
GREGORY KOLOVAKOS Literature Program Director, N.Y. State Council on the Arts
GARDNER McFALL Administrative Director, The Poetry Society of America

BOOK EDITORS SPEAK I: PUBLISHING POETRY

February 8   Panel Discussion

KATHY ANDERSON Associate Editor, W.W. Norton & Co.
MICHAEL BRAZILLER Co-founder and Publisher, Persea Books, Inc.
DENNIS COOPER Poet; Publisher, Little Caesar Press
PAT STRACHAN Executive Editor, Farrar, Straus & Giroux
BILL ZAVATSKY Poet; Publisher, Sun, a literary journal and independent publishing company

PUBLISHING POETRY BOOKS

February 15   Free Workshop

BOOK EDITORS SPEAK II: PUBLISHING FICTION AND NONFICTION

February 22   Panel Discussion

MARYA DALRYMPLE Senior Editor, Stewart, Tabori & Chang Publishers
STARLING LAWRENCE Vice President and Editor, W.W. Norton & Co.
ERROLL McDONALD Editor, Random House
ANN PATTY Editor-in-Chief, Poseidon Press
BARNEY ROSSET Founder and President, Grove Press, Inc.
PAM THOMAS Senior Editor, Crown Publishers

PUBLISHING FICTION AND NONFICTION BOOKS

March 1   Free Workshop

THE WRITERS UNION

March 8   Panel Discussion

Writers and representatives will discuss the feasibility, progress, and plans of The Writers Union.

ANNOTATED FILMOGRAPHY

POETS AND WRITERS ON FILM

It is important to be aware that there is valuable documentation of poets and writers on film. In 1981 two poets, Michael Scholnick and Jeff Wright, organized a series of screenings of selected "Poetry in Films," cosponsored by Millennium Film Workshop, Inc., and Teachers and Writers, with funds by the New York City Department of Employment. We are reprinting the list so it may be used as a resource.

William Carlos Williams. Selected readings from letters and poems and the autobiography of the poet are accompanied by illustrative scenes. Produced by Brice Howard in 1966 for National Educational Television. B/W, 10 minutes.

Robert Duncan and John Weiners. We look over Robert Duncan's shoulder as he writes parts of a long work-in-progress called "Passages Nigh." In the second half of the film, Duncan introduces us to John Weiners, and we go with the two poets to a torn-up room in the then-to-be-torn-down Hotel Wentley in San Francisco. Produced in 1966 for National Educational Television. B/W, 30 minutes.

Vladimir Nabokov. Living with his wife in Montreux, Switzerland, Vladimir Nabokov holds his first filmed interview. Directed by Robert Hughes and Terence McCarthy in 1966 for National Educational Television. B/W, 29 minutes.

Robert Creeley. The poet is shown with his wife, Bobbie, and their two young daughters in the adobelike house they shared in 1966 while he was poet-in-residence at the University of New Mexico. Produced in 1966 by Richard Meere for National Educational Television. B/W, 29 minutes.

John Berryman. I DON'T THINK I WILL SING ANY MORE JUST NOW. A documentary tracing the life and work of John Berryman. Produced by Carol Johnsen. Color, 30 minutes.

PULL MY DAISY. Jack Kerouac narrates his own prose poem. All-star cast. Produced and directed by Robert Frank and Al Leslie. 1959. B/W, 29 minutes.

Charles Olson. MAXIMUS TO HIMSELF. Filmed at Olson's home in Gloucester, Massachusetts. Produced by Theodora Cichy and William David Sherman. 1967. B/W with color sequences, 5 minutes.

T. S. Eliot. THE MYSTERIOUS MR. ELIOT. Produced jointly by the BBC and WNET. Reminiscences from Robert Lowell, Stephen Spender, I. A. Richards, Laurens Van Der Post, and Valerie Fletcher, Eliot's second wife. Matched with these interviews are film segments of Eliot reading from *The Four Quartets* and from rarely performed plays. Narrated by Keir Dullea. Color, 62 minutes.

Allen Ginsberg. SEPTEMBER ON JESSORE ROAD. Filmed traveling through Bangladesh. Soundtrack includes "September on Jessore Road" tuned and set to music with Allen Ginsberg, Happy Traum, and Bob Dylan. Color, 10 minutes.

D. H. Lawrence. D. H. LAWRENCE IN TAOS. Taos, New Mexico, the desert town where Lawrence lived in the 1920s and where his ashes repose today. British director Peter Davis focuses his camera on townspeople, including artist Dorothy Prett, who vied for Lawrence's affections half a century ago. Excerpts from his writings and lectures are shown. Color, 41 minutes.

Robert Frost. A LOVER'S QUARREL WITH THE WORLD. A warm, candid Frost is shown, full of homey wisdom, though his darker side is never far from the surface. Directed by Shirley Clarke. B/W, 40 minutes.

Louis Zukofsky. Explains underlying form and philosophy of his poetry. Produced in 1966 by Richard Moore for National Educational Television. B/W, 30 minutes.

Vladimir Mayakovsky. MAYAKOVSKY: THE POETRY OF ACTION. A vivid glimpse, focusing on his life as a revolutionary. Relevant old clips, and even a rare recording of Mayakovsky reading. Produced by Harold Mantell. Color, 22 minutes.

Frank O'Hara and Ed Sanders. O'Hara, shown in his workshop, reads. Sanders discusses pacifism and reads in his bookstore on the Lower East Side of New York. Produced by Richard Moore in 1966 for National Educational Television. B/W, 30 minutes.

Ezra Pound. Discusses his belief in the poetry of all things. A profile of Ezra Pound at his daughter's castle in Italy. Originally produced for the BBC. B/W, 15 minutes.

Gertrude Stein. WHEN THIS YOU SEE, REMEMBER ME. A portrait of this legendary author. Produced and directed by Perry Miller Adato. Color, 89 minutes.

THE BLUES ACCORDING TO LIGHTNIN' HOPKINS. 1968. Gritty documentary and red Texas earth. Directed by Les Blank.

Isaac Bashevis Singer. ISAAC SINGER'S NIGHTMARE & MRS. PUPKO'S BEARD. The author weaves in and out of one of his fictional creations. Produced by Brice Davidson. Color, 30 minutes.

Many filmmakers and film distributors have been interested in recording writers. Thorough research work could uncover a wealth of films of interest to you.

Sources:

Educational Film Library Association
43 West 63rd Street
New York, NY 10023
(212) 246-4533

Film Library
Donnell Library
20 West 53rd Street
New York, NY 10019
(212) 621-0609

ANNOTATED BIBLIOGRAPHY

Annual Registry of Grant Support, 1981-82. Marquis Academic Media, 200 East Ohio Street, Room 5615, Chicago, IL 60611 (about $55.00) Detailed information about a wide variety of support opportunities. Covers where to apply for funds for research, study, construction, library and literary programs, along with step-by-step guides to planning and proposal preparation that helps you anticipate and tailor your proposals to the specific requirements of each organization.

The Business of Being a Writer, by Stephen Goldman and Kathleen Sky. Harper & Row Publishers, Inc., New York, 1982. Help on legal, contractual, and other publishing matters affecting writers.

DIRECTORY OF PUBLISHING OPPORTUNITIES IN JOURNALS AND PERIODICALS. 4th edition, 1979. Marquis Academic Media, Marquis Who's Who, Inc., 200 East Ohio Street, Chicago, IL 60611. Directory of journals and periodicals under specialized field of study and discipline. Description of each publication's articles and editorial preferences, manuscript requirements, payments, and names of editors to address.

DRAMATISTS SOURCEBOOK, 1981-82 edition. Formerly published as *Information for Playwrights.* Theatre Communications Group, Inc., 355 Lexington Avenue, New York, NY 10017. Nationwide coverage of opportunities for playwrights, with a chapter on developmental theater and lists of theaters that read unsolicited manuscripts. Also includes information on script services, membership and service organizations, useful publications, colonies, fellowships and grants, state arts councils, college and university programs, media (film, radio, and TV), and new markets for plays. $6.95, softcover.

GADNEY'S GUIDE TO 1800 INTERNATIONAL CONTESTS, FESTIVALS AND GRANTS in Film & Video, Photography, TV-Radio Broadcasting, Writing, Poetry, Playwriting, and Journalism. Festival Publications, P.O. Box 10180, Glendale, CA 91209. For price, write to the above address. This book is frequently found in libraries and resource centers. Its chapter on writing and print journalism contains comprehensive information on fellowships, grants, colonies, and conferences.

Fear of Filing: A Tax Guide for Individual Artists. Volunteer Lawyers for the Arts, 1560 Broadway, Suite 711, New York, NY 10036. A step-by-step guide to preparing and filing tax returns for writers and artists.

Foundation Grants to Individuals. The Foundation Center, 888 Seventh Avenue, New York, NY 10106. This directory lists approximately 950 scholarships, fellowships, residencies, internships, grants, loans, awards, prizes, and other forms of assistance administered by private foundations.

How to Enter and Win Non-Fiction Writing Contests and *How to Enter and Win Fiction Writing Contests,* by Alan Gadney. Facts-on-File, New York.

HOW TO GET HAPPILY PUBLISHED, by Nancy Evans and Judith Applebaum, Plume Publishers ($5.95). Covers questions such as how to find an agent, best forms for a proposal, how to write cover letters, and how to direct your material to the right type of publisher. It also covers areas such as overseeing the publication process, self-promoting your work, and dealing with contracts. It includes a "Resources" list of all the people, places, books, and organizations that can help make publishing happily successful.

HOW TO WRITE LIKE A PRO, by Barry Tarshis, NAL Books ($10.95). Covers learning the specific writing techniques the pros know in order to write smoothly, clearly, and engagingly. You will learn how to organize, shape, and stage the flow of your material, and you will discover the best ways to use description and dialogue and what to do to direct the reader's attention to where you want it to go. Includes analysis of writing samples from great professionals and not-so-great student writers.

INTERNATIONAL DIRECTORY OF LITTLE MAGAZINES AND SMALL PRESSES, edited by Len Fulton and Ellen Ferber. 17th edition, 1981-1982. Dustbooks, P.O. Box 100, Paradise, CA 95969. Entries on small presses and little magazines include information on editorial personnel, subject interest, preferences, whether or not unsolicited manuscripts are accepted, price of sample and single issues, and subscription rates. Of utmost importance to writers submitting their work to such organizations.

LITERARY AND LIBRARY PRIZES, revised and edited by Olga S. Weber and Stephen J. Calvert. 10th edition, 1980. R. R. Bowker Company, New York & London, 1980. Chapter division falls into International, American, British, and Canadian prizes. Chapter on American prizes lists the following categories: General, Publishers, Juvenile, Poetry, Drama, Short Story, and Library (for library service). This book lists the history of each prize's recipients since its founding date, along with guidelines, cash awards given, and address.

Literary Market Place—The Directory of American Book Publishing. Published annually by R. R. Bowker Company, New York. The *LMP* lists names and numbers of American book publishing companies, agents, artists, and arts services, book clubs, book lists, book reviewers, calendar of trade events, columnists and commentators, courses for the book trade, editorial services, and other information essential to writers and publishers.

Money Business: Grants and Awards for Creative Artists by The Artists Foundation, Inc., 100 Boylston Street, Boston, MA 02116. $9.50. Descriptions of funding sources and artist colonies and exchange programs nationwide.

THE PUBLISH-IT-YOURSELF HANDBOOK: LITERARY TRADITION AND HOW-TO, edited by Bill Henderson. Pushcart Press and Harper & Row Publishers, Inc., 1973. Revised edition, 1980 ($12.50). Collection of essays and articles on and by small publishers, including Anais Nin, Leonard Woolf (Hogarth Press), Dick Higgins, and Richard Kostelanetz.

Theatre Directory, available from the Theatre Communications Group, 355 Lexington Avenue, New York, NY 10017. This annual pocket-sized directory provides at-a-glance information on more than 200 nonprofit professional theaters and related service organizations. $3.95, postpaid.

Translation & Translators: An International Directory and Guide edited by Stefan Congrat-Butlar. R. R. Bowker, New York. $35, cloth. Directory for the professional community of translators and support organizations. Contains listings of associations, centers, awards, fellowships, and grants.

The Writer's Legal Guide, by Tad Crawford. Volunteer Lawyers for the Arts, 1560 Broadway, Suite 711, New York, NY 10036. This book contains chapters on the new copyright laws; the general rights of the writer; contracts with agents, publishers, and producers; marketing information; vanity presses; income taxation; estate planning; and public support for writers. Also included are lists of lawyers' groups assisting artists and state arts agencies. $11, cloth.

1983 WRITERS MARKET, compiled by P. J. Schemenaur and John Brady. Published by Writer's Digest Books, 9933 Alliance Road, Cincinnati, OH 45242. A description and listing of all markets for writers—from advertising; book publishers; greeting cards; trade, technical, and professional journals; and creative writing. Lists book and magazine publishers, small and large, and corporations. Also included is a list of authors' agents.

The Writer's Survival Guide, by Jean Rosenbaum and Meryl Rosenbaum. Writer's Digest Books, New York. Help for the psyche of a writer.

Periodicals of Interest to Writers:

PUBLISHERS WEEKLY
R. R. Bowker Company
1180 Avenue of the Americas
New York, NY 10036
(212) 764-5100

The trade magazine of the publishing industry, *Publishers Weekly* is available at $38 per year (52 issues). Since it covers more than most writers and the average reader need to know, it is not sold at newsstands or bookstores; single copies may be bought for $2 only from the Bowker office. Most libraries subscribe; consult your library's reference or periodical section.

THE WRITER
The Writer, Inc.
8 Arlington Street
Boston, MA 02116
(617) 536-7420

Subscription: $12 per year (12 issues)
Single copy: $1
News for writers in all fields, with emphasis on marketing and writing technique.

WRITER'S DIGEST
9933 Alliance Road
Cincinnati, OH 45242
(513) 984-0710

Subscription: $18 per year (12 issues)
Single copy: $1.50
News for writers in all fields, with emphasis on marketing and writing technique.

Alphabetical Index of Organizations

Academy of American Poets, 13–14

Alliance of Literary Organizations, 15

American Indian Community House Gallery, 57

American Poetry Archives, 167

American Society of Journalists and Authors, 16–17

Artists Career Planning Service, 96

Associated Writing Programs, 97

Association of Hispanic Arts, Inc., 85–86

Authors Guild, Inc., 46–47

Authors League of America, Inc., 46–47

Basement Workshop, Inc., 58

Bronx Council on the Arts, 76

Brooklyn Arts and Cultural Association, 77–78

Center for Arts Information, 87–88

Center for Book Arts, 18–19

Center for Inter-American Relations, 59

Change, Inc., 108

Cintas Fellowship Program, 109

Committee of Small Magazine Editors and Publishers, 164

Coordinating Council of Literary Magazines, 20–22

Creative Artists Public Service Program, 110–111

Dramatists Guild, Inc., 48–49

Fiction Collective, 23

Foundation Center, 89–90

Foundation for the Community of Artists, 91–92

Frank Silvera Writers' Workshop, 61–62

Frederick Douglass Creative Arts Center, Inc., 63

Frederick Lewis Allen Memorial Room, 145

Giorno Poetry Systems Institute, Inc., 166

Graduate Writing Programs, 125–36

Greek Cultural Center, 64

El Grupo Morivivi, Inc., 60

Harlem Cultural Council, 79

Harlem Writers Guild, 65

Heresies Collective, Inc., 66

International Women's Writing Guild, 67

Lower Manhattan Cultural Council, 80

Manhattan Theatre Club, 168

Midmarch Associates, 68

National Association of Third World Writers, 50

National Endowment for the Arts, 112–113

National Scholarship Research Service, 114

National Writers Union, 51–52

New Wilderness Foundation, 24–25, 169

New York Area Media Alliance, 53

New York City Department of Cultural Affairs, 26

New York City Poetry Calendar, 170

New York City Urban Corps, 98

New York Feminist Art Institute, 69

New York State Artists-in-Residence Program, 99

New York State Council on the Arts' Internship/Apprenticeship Program, 100

New York State Council on the Arts, Literature Program, 115–118

Ollantay Center for the Arts, 70

Opportunity Resources for the Arts, 101

PEN American Center, 27–30

Poetry Center of the 92nd Street Y, 31–32

Poetry Project at St. Mark's Church in-the-Bowery, 33

Poetry Project Tape Collection, 170

Poetry Society of America, 34–35

Poets & Writers, Inc., 36–37

Poets in the Schools, 102

Print Center, Inc., 38

Publishing Center for Cultural Resources, 39

Queens Council on the Arts, 81–82

Rewrite, 92

Script Development Workshop, 103

Small Press and Magazine Distributors, 159–163

Small presses and magazines, 147–163

Snug Harbor Cultural Center, 145

Society of Authors' Representatives, 40

Staten Island Council on the Arts, 83

Teachers and Writers Collaborative, 104

Theatre Communications Group, 41–42

Translation Center, 43

Villager, 171

Village Voice/"Spoken Word," 171

Visual Studies Workshop, 44

Volunteeer Lawyers for the Arts, 54

"Where We At" Black Women Artists, Inc., 71

Women's Interart Center, 72–73

Women's Salon, 74

Writers' colonies, 138–144

Writers Community Inc., 105–106

Writers' conferences, 119–124

Writers Guild of America, East, Inc., 55

Writers Room, Inc., 146

Writers' Studio/Mercantile Library, 146

Index of Organizations by Subject

Agents
  "Advice from an Agent,"
    173–174
  Coordinating Council of Literary
    Magazines, 20–22
  Dramatists Guild, Inc., 48–49
  International Women's Writing
    Guild, 67
  Poets & Writers, Inc., 36–37
  Society of Authors'
    Representatives, 40
American Indian
  American Indian Community
    House Gallery, 57
  Arts Publico Press, 153
  Greenfield Review Press, 154
  Maize Press, 155
  Montana Council for Indian
    Education, 155
  Wood Ibis, 159
Apprenticeships and internships
  Basement Workshop, Inc., 58
  Center for Arts Information,
    87–88
  Coordinating Council of Literary
    Magazines, 20–22
  Fiction Collective, 23
  Greek Cultural Center, 64
  Heresies Collective, Inc., 66
  Manhattan Theatre Club, 168
  New Wilderness Foundation,
    24–25, 169
  New York City Department of

  Cultural Affairs/Arts
    Apprenticeship Program, 26
  New City Urban Corps, 98
  New York Feminist Art Institute,
    69
  New York State
    Artists-in-Residence Program,
    99
  New York State Council on the
    Arts' Internship/
    Apprenticeship Program, 100
  Teachers and Writers
    Collaborative, 104
  Visual Studies Workshop, 44
  Women's Interart Center, 72–73
  Women's Salon, 74
Asian American
  Asian American Studies Center,
    153
  Basement Workshop, Inc., 58
  Bridge: Asian American
    Perspectives, 153
  East Wind Magazine, 154
  El Grupo Morivivi, Inc., 60
  SEZ, 157
  Sunbury, 158
Awards and prizes
  Academy of American Poets,
    13–14
  Associated Writing Programs, 97
  Coordinating Council of Literary
    Magazines, 20–22
  PEN American Center, 27–30

Poetry Center of the 92nd Street
Y, 31–32
Poetry Society of America, 34–35
Translation Center, 43

Blacks
Brooklyn Arts and Cultural
Association, 77–78
New Paul Robeson Cultural
Center, 78
Universal Black Writer, The, 78
Frank Silvera Writers' Workshop,
61–62
Frederick Douglass Creative Arts
Center, Inc., 63
El Grupo Morivivi, Inc., 60
Harlem Cultural Council, 79
Harlem Writers Guild, 65
National Association of Third
World Writers, 50
National Writers Union, 51–52
SEZ, 157
Sunbury, 158
"Where We At" Black Women
Artists, Inc., 71
Wood Ibis, 159
Bronx: Bronx Council on the Arts,
76
Brooklyn
Brooklyn Arts and Cultural
Association, 77–78
"Where We At" Black Women
Artists, Inc., 71

Career and job information
American Society of Journalists
and Authors, 16–17
Artists Career Planning Service,
96
Associated Writing Programs, 97
Center for Arts Information,
87–88
Coordinating Council of Literary
Magazines, 20–22
Dramatists Guild, Inc., 48–49

Foundation for the Community
of Artists, 91–92
International Women's Writing
Guild, 67
New Wilderness Foundation,
24–25, 169
New York City Department of
Cultural Affairs, 26
New York City Urban Corps,
98
New York State
Artists-in-Residence Program,
99
New York State Council on the
Arts, 100, 115–118
Opportunity Resources for the
Arts, 101
PEN American Center, 27–30
Poets & Writers, Inc., 36–37
Poets in the Schools, 102
Queens Council on the Arts,
81–82
Script Development Workshop,
103
"Special Issues in Developing a
Writing Career," 173–174
Teachers and Writers
Collaborative, 104
Writers Community, Inc.,
105–106
College and university student
services and programs
Academy of American Poets,
13–14
Associated Writing Programs, 97
Coordinating Council of Literary
Magazines, 20–22
New York City Department of
Cultural Affairs/Arts
Apprenticeship Program, 26
Poetry Society of America,
34–35
Colonies and residencies, 137–144
Dramatists Guild, Inc., 48–49
Poets & Writers, Inc., 36–37

188

Conferences, symposia, and seminars
Alliance of Literary
Organizations, 15
American Society of Journalists
and Authors, 16–17
Associated Writing Programs, 97
Authors Guild, Inc., 46–47
Coordinating Council of Literary
Magazines, 20–22
Dramatists Guild, Inc., 48–49
Harlem Writers Guild, 65
International Women's Writing
Guild, 67
Midmarch Associates, 68
National Writers Union, 51–52
New York Area Media Alliance,
53
PEN American Center, 27–30
Teachers and Writers
Collaborative, 104
Translation Center, 43
Women's Interart Center, 72–73
Writers' conferences in the
Northeast, 119–124
Contests
Academy of American Poets,
13–14
Coordinating Council of Literary
Magazines, 20–22
PEN American Center, 27–30
Poetry Center of the 92nd Street
Y, 31–32
Cuban: Cintas Fellowship Program,
109

Emergency financial assistance
American Society of Journalists
and Authors, 16–17
Center for Arts Information,
87–88
Change, Inc., 108
Coordinating Council of Literary
Magazines, 20, 22
PEN American Center, 27–30

Exhibitions
Center for Book Arts, 18–19
Coordinating Council of Literary
Magazines, 20–22

Fiction
Basement Workshop, Inc., 58
Bronx Council on the Arts, 76
Fiction Collective, 23
Greek Cultural Center, 64
Harlem Writers Guild, 65
National Association of Third
World Writers, 50
National Writers Union, 51–52
PEN American Center, 27–30
Poetry Center of the 92nd Street
Y, 31–32
Poets & Writers, Inc., 36–37
Teachers and Writers
Collaborative, 104
Women's Salon, 74
Writers Community Inc.,
105–106
See also "Small Presses and
Magazines," 147–164

Grammar information: Rewrite, 92
Grants information
Academy of American Poets,
13–14
Bronx Council on the Arts, 76
Brooklyn Arts and Cultural
Association, 77–78
Change, Inc., 108
Cintas Fellowship Program, 109
Coordinating Council of Literary
Magazines, 20–22
Creative Artists Public Service
Program, 110–111
Dramatists Guild, Inc., 48–49
Fiction Collective, 23
Foundation Center, 89–90
Harlem Cultural Council, 79
National Association of Third
World Writers, 50

189

National Endowment for the Arts, 112–113
National Scholarship Research Service, 114
New York State Council on the Arts, Literature Program, 115–118
PEN American Center, 27–30
Poets & Writers, Inc., 36–37
Poets in the Schools, 102
Queens Council on the Arts, 81–82
Translation Center, 43
Writers Guild of America, East, Inc., 55
See also "Annotated Bibliography," 178–182
Greek: Greek Cultural Center, 64

Health benefits
American Society of Journalists and Authors, 16–17
Dramatists Guild, Inc., 48–49
Foundation for the Community of Artists, 91–92
New York Area Media Alliance, 53
High school students and children
Bronx Council on the Arts, 76
Brooklyn Arts and Cultural Association, 77–78
Lollipop Power, Inc., 155
Poetry Center of the 92nd Street Y, 31–32
Poets in the Schools, 102
Queens Council on the Arts, 81–82
Teachers and Writers Collaborative, 104
Hispanics
Arts Publico Press, 153
Association of Hispanic Arts, Inc., 85–86
Center for Arts Information, 87–88

Center for Inter-American Relations, 59
Coordinating Council of Literary Magazines, 20–22
El Grupo Morivivi, Inc., 60
Harlem Writers Guild, 65
Maize Press, 155
National Association of Third World Writers, 50
National Writers Union, 51–52
Ollantay Center for the Arts, 70
Poets & Writers, Inc., 36–37
Queens Council on the Arts, 81–82
Review, 156
SEZ, 157
Women's Salon, 74

International programs
Center for Book Arts, 18–19
International Women's Writing Guild, 67
New Wilderness Foundation, 24–25, 169
PEN American Center, 27–30
Poetry Project at St. Mark's Church in-the-Bowery 33
Visual Studies Workshop, 44
"Where We At" Black Women Artists, Inc., 71
Women's Salon, 74
Writers Guild of America, East, Inc., 55
Italian-American: El Grupo Morivivi, Inc., 60

Legal Advice
Authors Guild, Inc., 46–47
Authors League of America, 46–47
Dramatists Guild, Inc., 48–49
National Writers Union, 51–52
PEN American Center, 27–30
Poets & Writers, Inc., 36–37

Volunteer Lawyers for the Arts, 54

Writers Guild of America, East, Inc., 55

Libraries and archives
American Poetry Archives, 167
Basement Workshop, Inc., 58
Center for Arts Information, 87–88
Coordinating Council of Literary Magazines, 20–22
Dramatists Guild, Inc., 48–49
Foundation Center, 89–90
Frank Silvera Writers' Workshop, 61–62
Giorno Poetry Systems Institute, Inc., 166
New Wilderness Foundation, 24–25, 169
New York Feminist Art Institute, 69
Poetry Center of the 92nd Street Y, 31–32
Poetry Project Tape Collection, 170
Poetry Society of America, 34–35
Visual Studies Workshop, 44
See also "Annotated Filmography," 176–178

Literary bookstores and distributors
National Association of Third World Writers, 50
Poets & Writers, Inc.: *Literary Bookstores: A List in Progress,* 37
Publishing Center for Cultural Resources, 39
Visual Studies Workshop, 44
See also "Small Press and Magazine Distributors," 159–163

Mailing lists: Poets & Writers, Inc., 36–37

Minority services and information
American Indian Community House Gallery, 57
Association of Hispanic Arts, Inc., 85–86
Basement Workshop, Inc., 58
Center for Inter-American Relations, 59
Coordinating Council of Literary Magazines, 20–22
Frederick Douglass Creative Arts Center, Inc., 63
Greek Cultural Center, 64
El Grupo Morivivi, Inc., 60
Harlem Cultural Council, 79
Harlem Writers Guild, 65
National Association of Third World Writers, 50
New Wilderness Foundation, 24–25, 169
Ollantay Center for the Arts, 70
Poets & Writers, Inc., 36–37
Women's Salon, 74

Multi-arts: Women's Interart Center, 72–73

Multimedia: New Wilderness Foundation, 24–25, 169

Newsletters, bulletins, and calendars
Academy of American Poets, 13–14
Associated Writing Programs, 97
Association of Hispanic Arts, Inc., 85–86
Authors Guild, Inc., 46–47
Bronx Council on the Arts, 76
Brooklyn Arts and Cultural Association, 77–78
Coordinating Council of Literary Magazines, 20–22
Dramatists Guild, Inc., 48–49
Foundation for the Community of Artists, 91–92
Frank Silvera Writers' Workshop, 61–62

Frederick Douglass Creative Arts
  Center, Inc., 63
International Women's Writing
  Guild, 67
Lower Manhattan Cultural
  Council, 80
National Association of Third
  World Writers, 50
National Endowment for the
  Arts, 112–113
New Wilderness Foundation,
  24–25, 169
New York Area Media Alliance,
  53
PEN American Center, 27–30
Poetry Project at St. Mark's
  Church in-the-Bowery, 33
Poetry Society of America, 34–35
Poets & Writers, Inc., 36–37
Queens Council on the Arts,
  81–82
Staten Island Council on the
  Arts, 83
Volunteeer Lawyers for the Arts,
  54
Writers Community Inc., 105–106
Nonfiction
  Alliance of Literary
    Organizations, 15
  American Society of Journalists
    and Authors, 16–17
  Bronx Council on the Arts, 76
  Frederick Douglass Creative Arts
    Center, Inc., 63
  International Women's Writing
    Guild, 67
  National Writers Union, 51–52
  New York Area Media Alliance,
    53

Organizations outside New York
  City
  American Poetry Archives, San
    Francisco, 167

International Women's Writing
  Guild, Saratoga Springs, NY,
  67
National Endowments of the
  Arts, Washington, DC,
  112–113
National Scholarship Research
  Service, San Rafael, CA, 114
Visual Studies Workshop,
  Rochester, NY, 44

Playwrighting
  American Indian Community
    House Gallery, 57
  Basement Workshop, Inc., 58
  Dramatists Guild, Inc., 48–49
  Frank Silvera Writers' Workshop,
    61–62
  Frederick Douglass Creative Arts
    Center, Inc., 63
  Harlem Writers Guild, 65
  International Women's Writing
    Guild, 67
  National Association of Third
    World Writers, 50
  Ollantay Center for the Arts, 70
  PEN American Center, 27–30
  Poetry Center of the 92nd Street
    Y, 31–32
  Script Development Workshop,
    103
  Society of Authors'
    Representatives, 40
  Theatre Communications Group,
    41–42
  Women's Interart Center,
    72–73
Poetry
  Academy of American Poets,
    13–14
  Antaeus, 149
  Basement Workshop, Inc., 58
  Bronx Council on the Arts, 76
  Chelsea Magazine, 150

Ecco Press, 149
Full Court Press, 150
El Grupo Morivivi, Inc., 60
International Women's Writing
  Guild, 67
National Writers Union, 51–52
New York Quarterly, 151
Paris Review, 151
Parnassus: Poetry in Review, 151
PEN American Center, 27–30
Poetry Center of the 92nd Street
  Y, 31–32
Poetry Project at St. Mark's
  Church in-the-Bowery, 33
Poetry Society of America,
  34–35
Poets & Writers, Inc., 36–37
Poets in the Schools, 102
Pulpsmith, 152
Sun and Moon Press, 157
Sun Press and *Sun Magazine,* 152
Writers Community, Inc.,
  105–106
Unmuzzled Ox, 152
Poetry readings
Academy of American Poets,
  13–14
American Indian Community
  House Gallery, 57
Basement Workshop, Inc., 58
Giorno Poetry Systems Institute,
  Inc., 166
El Grupo Morivivi, Inc., 60
Manhattan Theatre Club, 168
New Wilderness Foundation,
  24–25, 169
New York City Poetry Calendar,
  170
Poetry Center of the 92nd Street
  Y, 31–32
Poetry Project at St. Mark's
  Church in-the-Bowery, 33
Poetry Society of America, 34–35
Poets & Writers, Inc., 36–37

Villager, 171
Village Voice/"Spoken Words,"
  171
See also "Readings: Live and
  Recorded," 165–172
Prison writers' services
Greenfield Review Press, 154
PEN American Center, 27–30
Poetry Society of America, 34–35
Publications
Academy of American Poets,
  13–14
American Indian Community
  House Gallery, 57
American Society of Journalists
  and Authors, 16–17
Center for Arts Information,
  87–88
Center for Book Arts, 18–19
Center for Inter-American
  Relations, 59
Coordinating Council of Literary
  Magazines, 20–22
Dramatists Guild, Inc., 48–49
Fiction Collective, 23
Foundation Center, 89–90
Frederick Douglass Creative Arts
  Center, Inc., 63
Greek Cultural Center, 64
Heresies Collective, Inc., 66
Midmarch Associates, 68
New Wilderness Foundation,
  24–25, 169
New York City Department of
  Cultural Affairs, 26
Ollantay Center for the Arts, 70
PEN American Center, 27–30
Poetry Project at St. Mark's
  Church in-the-Bowery, 33
Poetry Society of America, 34–35
Poets & Writers, Inc., 36–37
Poets in the Schools, 102
Queens Council on the Arts,
  81–82

Society of Authors'
  Representatives, 40
Teachers and Writers
  Collaborative, 104
Theatre Communications Group,
  41–42
Translation Center, 43
Visual Studies Workshop, 44
Volunteer Lawyers for the Arts,
  54
"Where We At" Black Women
  Artists, Inc., 71
Publishing Information
  Bronx Council on the Arts, 76
  Center for Book Arts, 18–19
  Coordinating Council of Literary
    Magazines, 20–22
  Dramatists Guild, Inc., 48–49
  Fiction Collective, 23
  International Women's Writing
    Guild, 67
  National Association of Third
    World Writers, 50
  PEN American Center, 27–30
  Poets & Writers, Inc., 36–37
  Print Center, Inc., 38
  Publishing Center for Cultural
    Resources, 39
  Visual Studies Workshop, 44

Queens
  Greek Cultural Center, 64
  Ollantay Center for the Arts, 70
  Queens Council on the Arts,
    81–82

Readings
  Academy of American Poets,
    13–14
  Bronx Council on the Arts, 76
  Brooklyn Arts and Cultural
    Association, 77–78

Center for Book Arts, 18–19
Center for Inter-American
  Relations, 59
Coordinating Council of Literary
  Magazines, 20–22
Fiction Collective, 23
Frank Silvera Writers' Workshop,
  61–62
Greek Cultural Center, 64
El Grupo Morivivi, Inc., 60
Harlem Writers Guild, 65
Lower Manhattan Cultural
  Council, 80
New Wilderness Foundation,
  24–25, 169
New York City Poetry Calendar,
  170
Ollantay Center for the Arts, 70
PEN American Center, 27–30
Poetry Center of the 92nd Street
  Y, 31–32
Poetry Project at St. Mark's
  Church in-the-Bowery, 33
Poetry Society of America, 34–35
Poets & Writers, Inc., 36–37
Queens Council on the Arts,
  81–82
Women's Salon, 74
Writers Community, Inc., 105–106
See also Poetry readings;
  "Readings: Live and
  Recorded,"165–171

Senior citizens
  Bronx Council on the Arts, 76
  Brooklyn Arts and Cultural
    Association, 77–78

Staten Island
  Snug Harbor Cultural Center,
    145
  Staten Island Council on the
    Arts, 83

Television, radio, and screen writers
American Society of Journalists
and Authors, 16-17
Center for Inter-American
Relations, 57
Frederick Douglass Creative Arts
Center, Inc., 63
Greek Cultural Center, 64
New Wilderness Foundation,
24-25, 169
New York Area Media Alliance,
53
Script Development Workshop,
103
Theatre Communications Group,
41-42
Women's Interart Center, 72-73
Writers Guild of America, East,
Inc., Manuscript Registration
Service, 55
See also "Annotated
Filmography," 176-178

Translations
Academy of American Poets,
13-14
Center for Inter-American
Relations, 59
Logbridge, 155
National Endowment for the
Arts, 112-113

New York State Council on the
Arts, 115-118
PEN American Center, 27-30
Review, 156
Sun Press and Sun Magazine, 152
Theatre Communications Group,
41-42
Translation Center, 43

Women
Coordinating Council of Literary
Magazines, 20-22
Feminist Press, 154
Harlem Writers Guild, 65
Heresies Collective, Inc., 66
International Women's Writing
Guild, 67
Midmarch Associates, 68
National Association of Third
World Writers, 50
National Writers Union, 51-52
New York Feminist Art
Institute, 69
Persephone Press, Inc., 156
Spinsters, Inc., 157
Sunbury, 158
13th Moon, 158
"Where We At" Black Women
Artists, Inc., 71
Women's Interart Center, 72-73
Women's Salon, 74
Wood Ibis, 159